$\mathcal{W}$ILDFLOWERS —— AND —— TRAIN WHISTLES

Stories of a Coal Mining Family

LILLIAN "SISSY CRONE" FRAZER

EDITED BY: CHRISTY STEELE FRAZER

authorHOUSE®

AuthorHouse™
1663 Liberty Drive
Bloomington, IN 47403
www.authorhouse.com
Phone: 1 (800) 839-8640

Published by AuthorHouse 01/27/2018

ISBN: 978-1-5462-2656-7 (sc)
ISBN: 978-1-5462-2655-0 (e)

Library of Congress Control Number: 2018901282

Print information available on the last page.

Any people depicted in stock imagery provided by Thinkstock are models, and such images are being used for illustrative purposes only. Certain stock imagery © Thinkstock.

This book is printed on acid-free paper.

To my son J.J., my daughter Nikki and my family. . . my gifts from God.

1

FLOOD 2016

It's summer, the latter part of June 2016. Pictures of flooded homes and cars being washed away flash across the television screen. The flood of June 23 and 24 in the State of West Virginia has claimed at least 23 lives and counting. Palmer, his daughter Lilli, who has made her home with us for the last eleven years, and I sit in our suburban Virginia home watching the newscast. We are drawn to the television, hypnotized by the disaster.

Waves of sadness crash into us sitting helplessly in our cozy living room. I walk away to escape the pictures of devastation, only to go back to my watching spot bringing the waves crashing again. My heart goes out to the flood victims. I can relate to the victims, they live where I lived, floods and all. I shudder to think of what they are facing.

Listening to the news reports my mind drifts back in time to memories of other floods that my family and I lived through while growing up in the small coal town of Minden, West Virginia.

The flash floods on the television are real to me. I remember watching the water climb, praying for the rain to stop, feeling the anxiety set in when you realize the rain is not stopping, and seeing the flood waters rise in the streets eventually breeching houses.

We were lucky back then, the floods destroyed things, but not people. Today's flood is different; people are dying.

Ten inches of torrential rain continues to drown out the hills of West Virginia. Some people are surprised that mountainous geography can flood. It's the creeks and rivers that are overflowing with water running down the mountainsides. Flash floods are not new to the people living here.

Today's flood claims many homes and all the worldly possessions of the displaced families. Roads are washed out, bridges destroyed, and businesses damaged. Structures that will be salvaged are full of contaminated, brownish muddy water. Everything must be scrubbed and bleached. If history repeats itself, many of these families, if not most, have no insurance or at least not flood insurance. Flood insurance may not even be available in their areas.

The news focuses on a house in Greenbrier County that is dislodged from its foundation, floating down the river completely engulfed in flames fed by leaking propane. It's not the only floating house; pictures of decimated homes scroll one after another across the television screen.

A lonely man sits atop his trailer waiting to be rescued. The camera pans wider revealing he's one of many residents perched on trailer roofs waiting patiently for emergency responders. Without a boat there is nowhere to go. However, not all are so lucky, reporters are beginning to tell tales of the deceased and missing. Children are some of the victims who are swept away by the floodwaters.

The County of Greenbrier is in complete chaos and some areas look like a war zone. Much of what is shown on television is from Greenbrier County, adjacent to Fayette County, my childhood home. However, the devastation extends far beyond Greenbrier; 44 of 55 counties in West Virginia are declared a state of emergency with the National Guard deployed to perform rescue and security operations.

Tragedy has a way of bringing out the best in some and the worst in others. Trickling in are reports of West Virginians banding together to help each other, while opportunistic looters are also reported.

Dubbed by the broadcasts as the worst flooding for West Virginia in 100 years, I remember many times outsiders calling us "strong people," but I always hated that phrase, knowing for us it is not a matter of being strong but doing what must be done to survive mentally and physically. The victims of this flood are strong people, too, and I have full confidence that they will recover.

My phone rings bringing a welcome distraction from the television. My son J.J. is calling. He tells me that he and my daughter-in-law Christy and my grandsons Connor and Garrett will be able to attend the family reunion in West Virginia in a few weeks.

"Yes, that's right!" I exclaim. "I almost forgot about the reunion." Few family members live in West Virginia now, but we continue to have our reunions at one of the West Virginia state or county parks. We gleefully await our bi-annual family reunion; however, this year may be different. There is no news yet on whether the park picnic area will still be able to accommodate us. It might be affected by the flood.

My son John Michael, nicknamed J.J., is the constant in my life. He met his wife Christy while in college and now years later after graduation and marriage they own a thriving security business. Owning their own business means their personal plans often change at the last moment. I tell him he inherited the family trait of being a hard worker. I assured him we will have the reunion, even though I have a tiny flicker of doubt myself.

Finishing our conversation, I peer out the window with my childhood home in mind. There is little physical resemblance of my Minden home and this one. In suburbia, our family room has a soaring two-story ceiling with beautiful large arched windows surrounding a gas fireplace. The massive windows allow the outside to enter. Purchasing this house was one of my last real estate transactions prior to retiring from real estate. Palmer and I sold our homes with acreage to move closer to work and family. Now that we have a small parcel of land, we miss the acreage at fleeting moments. We traded our open acreage for a golf course community with access to bike trails, pools, and fishing ponds without the hassle of caring for them.

The summers are wonderful here. I look out to green grass and leafy trees with bushes and flowers bursting into bud. The sky is dark blue with scattered cotton clouds floating high above the trees. The gradual onset of dusk begins to crawl across the horizon and the sun sinks lower as the daylight inches away from us. At night when the moon is shining bright, it appears to be sitting in our family room through the undraped windows.

We have a distant view of Bull Run Mountain, the easternmost front of the Blue Ridge Mountain Range. Unlike us, time has not changed the soft ups and downs of the mountains. We are safe with peace and quiet so far away from the devastation aching in the heart of West Virginia.

My name is Lillian Crone Frazer. I am no longer a young girl in the coal town, but then again, a part of me will always be her. During my childhood in West Virginia, I was known as Sissy Crone, the baby of the family. I was the youngest of seven children, four boys and three girls.

Mom and dad, Elizabeth and Reginald Crone, known as Buster and Lizzy, were both born and raised in our little coal town. My maternal grandparents, born in Hungary, came to West Virginia directly after their arrival at Ellis Island. My paternal grandparents, German, Irish and English descendants, moved to West Virginia from fertile farm lands in neighboring Virginia. They did not earn fortunes in the coal fields, but they did make a decent living and provided homes for their families.

As for my siblings and I, although we are all individuals, it is difficult to think of myself without thinking of the other six or to think of one of them without thinking of the remainder of us. It seems we made a whole.

Buster Crone Family: Buster, Lizzy, Squeaky, Sue, Charles, Ann, Robert, John and Sissy. Each of us were born and raised in Minden.

My memories drift in and out of the forefront of my mind while watching the flood waters on the television. I'm normally calm, but today I'm too edgy to settle. I pace a bit as I think of our little coal town and the floods that happened there when I was young. I would like to say I loved our little town, but I didn't. My parents and big brother Squeaky did, but it was different for them than it was when the younger siblings were growing up. Although I didn't love the town, I did love its people.

There is no mistaking though, that our little coal town is a part of us whether we loved it or not. The hollers in the hills near Minden had a huge part in molding us, its simple virtues cling to us, the rocky dusty

5

roads lead us to our fair share of challenges. The vibrant wildflowers gave us beauty, the church gave us faith, and the miners represented work ethics.

I could say that our little coal camp town had rustic charm, but it did not. Coal towns seem to conjure up visions of dirty, poor and uneducated folks who are controlled and manipulated by the coal company, in accommodations not much better than living in a tent. From the outside looking in, perhaps that's what is seen. For certain coal towns are dirty. It is the nature of the beast. There is no escaping coal soot. And certainly, miners were at the mercy of the owners and coal company operators who were powerful and rich. My immediate and extended family were proud folks who worked hard and grabbed ahold of every opportunity afforded to us. We did not think of ourselves as the stereotypical coal camp family. There was a vibrancy to us that outsiders didn't see.

The town itself was owned and managed by the coal company and was more a community interwoven by communal buildings and private homes. In today's age, it's hard to imagine an entire town being owned by a single company. The coal company owners did not live in the town, only the miners, company employees, and their families. The coal company rented the homes to the miners, the rent was deducted from their pay.

The coal company acted as if they cared for the miners by providing access to living quarters and jobs, but they cared only for as long as they needed the miners and under their terms. By today's standards, in terms of monetary wealth we would be considered poor. But what we lacked in money, we were rich with childhood dreams. There were abundant, endless days of tagging along with my brothers, sisters and our friends tramping across the hollers, exploring caves, picking blackberries, walking the railroad tracks, listening to the chugging of the train and its deep whistle blows echoing throughout Oak Hill and Minden.

Eventually the coal camp era eroded with the innovation of modern technologies and the lack of coal. So, when the company no longer needed the town and its people, it was shuttered, and we were abandoned. The shutdown of the mines left everyone with fears of uncertainty. Once the mines closed, there were no jobs nearby and our home was sold by the coal company while we were still living in it.

The most disheartening reference made to me of our town was, "Did you live down in that hole?" to which I felt deserved no response. To an outsider, our hollers may appear bleak and despairing, even hopeless at times and surely uninviting. To us, it was home.

Minden ran about two miles long, but we included Rock Lick and Conchu as part of Minden, so it was a little longer. As a young girl, I often looked up to a hazy sky and the smell of Sulphur hovering in the air from the smoke rising over the burning slate dump that sat on one hillside. I can almost hear the coal train as the beast blows its whistle and rumbles down the railroad tracks, stopping and backing up and starting again as it picks up or drops off coal cars.

If there is a slight breeze, it carries the fragrance of the wild honeysuckle that grows along our fence into our play area. I gulp a deep breath of the sweet perfumed honeysuckle before rushing off to play with my brothers Squeaky, Charles, Robert and John, sisters Sue and Ann, and friends who are laughing and talking all at the same time.

Our town started off as bustling and prosperous, but by the late 1950s, the prosperity disappeared when the coal company abandoned us, leaving homeless coal miners in its wake. As a child I thought maybe someone broke a mirror and bestowed a seven-year bad luck curse upon us. It certainly seemed like bad luck to me. In the eyes of a child, it was easy enough to find out who broke the mirror, gather the pieces, and bury them in the moonlight to break the curse. Unfortunately, we never found the broken pieces, so the curse was our burden to bear for life.

2

HIGHWAY HOME

July 2016. The waters have receded from the historic 100-year flood that ravaged the state of West Virginia. The entire state is in recovery mode. We receive good news that the Holiday Lodge in Oak Hill is prepared to accommodate us during our Crone family reunion.

Palmer and I pack the GMC truck bed and back seats until they are practically overflowing with donations for the flood victims. Twenty-two years of my life were spent working at a labor law firm in Washington, D.C., and much of the donations I'm bringing to West Virginia are from my generous co-workers who opened their hearts to help those in need even though they knew no one directly impacted by the floods.

The truck is loaded with cases of bleach, soaps, food, diapers, dog food, and school supplies. I am electrified with anticipation of renewing kinship with family members I rarely see, as well as fulfilling my mission to help the flood victims.

During the packing I contemplate in my mind about why people go back to the same flood-prone land after the waters recede; why not start fresh outside the flood zone, further from the narrow creeks that are not deep enough or wide enough to hold the mountain rains? Why return? The answer is painfully simple — because where else would they go? It is their home, and it was home to us, too.

Our Appalachian roots are cemented in a bedrock of backaches, heartaches, and tragedies. The struggles of a hard life humbled us, and trained us to live our lives practically, hoping for the best but expecting the worst. Appalachians take to heart the saying, "If the good Lord is willing and the creeks don't rise" as a truism that served as our life's motto.

I grab my dog Spunky, a small mixed breed with an adorable face and a personality that goes with his name, and we hop in the truck riding "shotgun." I settle in for the ride with a book in my lap, sunglasses on, and listening to the country music station Palmer has blasting on the radio.

The road fades away as I think about my childhood home in Minden, nestled snugly in a holler only six or seven miles from the New River Gorge Bridge. This steel arch bridge is a West Virginia landmark with picturesque views of the surrounding mountains regardless of the season. It was the longest single-span arch bridge at its completion but has since lost this title. The bridge represents West Virginia on the state quarter and is a major tourist destination. Festivities on the bridge bring thousands of spectators each year including base jumpers and whitewater rafters who enjoy trailing down the New River.

We drive Route 66 towards West Virginia. It's a beautiful sunny day, and I am grateful for the bright morning. The mist and fogginess often draped over the mountain tops is gone, instead our windshield is filled with brilliant green hills. Layers of mountains lay before us. For some, mountains bring a feeling of melancholy, but for me they are serene with their vast peacefulness.

Palmer drives in silence as the highway leads us through countryside and valleys and stunning scenery. If it wasn't for the updated highways, this geography hasn't changed since my childhood.

Palmer grew up on a large farm as a mountain boy in Bath County, Virginia. He tells anyone and everyone, "Bath County has the best hunting and fishing a body can find," not that he does much of either these days. I think of the woods surrounding my childhood home, and don't recall seeing any deer or rabbits or any other animals. Local folklore is that during the Great Depression, hunters practically rid the hills of animals to feed their families, and the animal ecosystem hadn't recovered. Perhaps they have returned by now.

Palmer's prized tokens, his cherished deer heads, hang on our unfinished basement walls, the only place I agree they can be displayed. Other than us and grandsons Connor and Garrett, no one else has interest in our unfinished basement which houses a ping pong table, an old pool table, gym equipment and an outdated large screen television that still plays great.

When Connor and Garrett were little, they studied the deer heads on the wall with great concentration. The youngest, Garrett, finally asked in his youthful innocence, "How did the deer get stuck in the wall?" Both boys darted back and forth from inside to outside, trying to uncover the whereabouts of the other half of the deer, and didn't understand why or how someone could stuff a deer head. Raised in a suburban golf course community, Connor and Garrett haven't been exposed to many deer heads hanging on walls.

The recent flood in West Virginia has my thoughts flashing back again to the first flood of my childhood. Spontaneous flashes of memories linger in the back of my mind and jump out sometimes when I'm least expecting it.

Memories don't come back to me in chronological order, rather people, pictures, letters, smells or sounds trigger vignettes to play across my mind. These memories, like my closets, are cramped full and the treasured past falls out when a door is opened. Sometimes I look through my inner closet to remember what is stashed inside.

Some of the most valuable memories aren't what has happened to me directly, but rather are stories and reminiscences passed to me from family and friends. Our front porch was a haven for juicy gossip while we laughed and talked together.

In 1956, the coal camp era was beginning to decline. It is not the flood of my youth that haunts me, but rather the feeling of the unknown. Life as we knew it was coming to an end. Like my family, most families had no place to go and no job to support them. It is a gut knotting fear. As my mama said, "when it rains, it pours," which it did horrifically during the flood that washed away so many of our hangouts when we were kids.

These days are not ones filled with video games, fast food chain restaurants, cell phones and instant photos. Our telephones were shared lines which youngsters seldom used and photos were unnecessary luxuries taken rarely and often never developed because developing the film cost money we didn't have.

As my thoughts travel back, I can feel the early evening breeze flow through our little valley as the crickets sing inconsistent tunes and the faint light of the moon shines overhead. I hear the creak of the porch glider moving back and forth playing a tune of its own. The fireflies light up the sky as the mosquitoes fly around trying to find their next victim.

My memories are intertwined with the newspaper articles Mom collected. Mom and Dad were vigorous readers of local newspapers, and they saved many articles for our scrapbook. One of those articles was a poem "The Hard Way" by Ben Burroughs. This poem epitomizes much of our life. As I read it, I understood why Mama kept this poem.

Learn all you can as you traverse
The rocky roads of life
The hard way leads to happiness
The easy way to strife

Those years seem to bring one struggle after another, so we learned constantly on our rocky road.

I jump from my seat, Palmer pulling me from my day dreams when he spots wild turkey in the meadow. His excitement is overflowing as he looks at me through deep blue eyes and waves his arm and exclaims, "Did you see them? The turkey, did you see them?" He has eyes of a hawk when it comes to wild game.

Attempting to share his enthusiasm, I let out a long breath of air, responding in what I consider to be eagerness in my voice but it's not easy to get excited about wild turkey. "Yes, I see them!" I bellow.

3

WILDFLOWERS

July 1956. My family and I live bordering the paved road in Minden, a little coal mining town tucked in the mountains of Fayette County. When I say bordering, I truly mean very near the road as there is a small patch of yard between the house and the road, not enough to play or plant much of anything.

Obviously, the coal company didn't anticipate the "hard road" being built when they constructed these coal company houses in the days of our Grandpas. At times, I visualize a car going astray and landing into a house. (*That day will come years later.*)

To enter the town, you must go under a small covered bridge that allows only a single car to pass, so a car coming up the hill and one going down cannot enter at the same time. Most of us are accustomed to twisty roads that wind around our mountains. By comparison, our hill is not so steep and only a mile long, so the curves are not too severe. There are few guard rails, on the left side are tall rocky cliffs and the right side drops to land below. The other roads are made of red dog or dust dirt.

A view of Minden as you enter the town. Picture courtesy of Jane Webb Terry.

Near the top of this hill on the right-hand side sits a sewer plant that services Oak Hill, a neighboring town. One day, cousins of our friend Bill Harmon, who lived up the road from us, were exploring the upper end of Minden near the sewer plant. We don't know what they were doing exactly, but their dog fell into the sewer water holding pool. The boys were unable to pull the dog out, so one of them jumped in to rescue the pup. He couldn't let his dog drown in all that mess. For years afterwards, people still chuckled in disgust at the thought of a coal camp kid jumping into the sewer plant.

Many days the gray mist and fog settle over our little valley on early mornings. It is often late morning before the mighty sun peeks through the mist awakening our town, sunrays piercing the hill adding glorious color to our world of dreary coal camp life.

Our hillside town has no lush bottomlands, no cattle grazing, no historical buildings, no white picket fences or neatly manicured lawns. Coal camp houses, once white, are now trimmed in black soot and coal dust giving them a grayish appearance. Coal dust creeps inside the houses constantly.

Behind the houses on the right side of the road runs the muddy creek of Arbuckle, usually a small narrow stream of water with a shallow bed. The creek has a brownish flow because it carries the run off from the mines. During heavy downpours, the Arbuckle creek overflows easily. Our parents told us to stay away from the creek, "Who knows what runs into the creek," we hear them say. Others say, "Some families run their sewer lines into the creek."

The coal town water company brings water from a spring near the mines, but as kids we thought that the water came from the mines. One of my brothers finally told me that the spring is separate from the mines. (*Both the water source and the sewer changed in the 1970s.*)

On the other side of the creek running parallel is the railroad track where a massive train delivers the town mail, supplies, and people in and out of town. Most importantly the train transports our coal.

I love the sound of the train as the whistles blow long and loud and the grinding noises of the steel grow as the engine stops and starts again, loading and unloading cars. You can feel the vibrations of the train and hear the clacking of the coal cars as it rolls down the track. The houses, some on stilts, shook from the train's movements.

Our neighbors are immigrants from various nationalities. The coal companies needed miners, and the immigrants freshly deposited on Ellis Island, like our Grandpa Vegh, were prime candidates to lure to the dusty roads of a coal camp. The mines also enticed farmers, like my Grandpa Crone, African Americans, and mountain men. The chorus of diverse speech, some in a slow dialect of Appalachian slang, and others with heavy accents speaking broken English or no English, melded together in a sing-song melody heard throughout the hills.

Although we are a diverse town, we don't seem to notice that much. After all, you rely on one another regardless of ethnicity down in the mine shafts; it takes all people working together to come back alive.

Our hair is rather unstylish, and our smiles imperfect. Clothes and shoes worn daily are faded hand-me-downs, but we do have a couple nicer outfits to wear to school and on special occasions, like Christmas.

We have a large family and there are many to buy for so new clothes are limited. Although we have few material items, Mama and Daddy take pride in our home, reminding us that we are respectable and hard-working people.

There is an intimacy among the coal camp people, a bond of friendship and hardship shared. This type of bonding welds people together. There is a common choreography to coal camp life; Mamas hanging worn and sun faded laundry out to dry on lines strung from poles across the back or side yards, dusty and dirty dogs running alongside their young masters, kids playing in the street. Repeatedly, day in and day out, the routine recurs in harmony with the clickety clack of the train coming down the track.

Minden Road continues down the holler to Rock Lick and Conchu. I can't understand why they are named differently, as one area blends into the other, and both share a post office and a school. Daddy says they are named different towns because of the mines. Rock Lick and Conchu each had a coal mine at one time as well as Minden.

At the far reaches of Conchu, there is beautiful undisturbed land with mirrored ponds, hidden far back between tall trees. "No trespassing" signs are posted which makes us even more curious to see what exists beyond the signs. We didn't know at the time, but our "Wonderland" became home to Ace Adventure Resort, a famous whitewater rafting and outdoor adventure destination.

Wild honeysuckle vines are prevalent in town and are my favorite. Our postage stamp-sized yard has many honeysuckle vines covering the wire fence, filling the air with a sweet perfumed scent, which helps block out the burned gunpowder smell hovering over the slate dump near our home.

The slate dump is huge, taller than some of the surrounding hills. My brothers say the slate dump smells like rotten eggs. While I can't recall smelling rotten eggs, I do remember the Sulfuric smells of burning slate nastily hanging over our house. My brothers go to the slate dump to collect pieces of discarded coal for our fireplace. The fireplace and the kitchen potbelly stove are our only heat sources. At times, my sisters and I go with the boys to the slate dump, but it gives me a creepy feeling. To me, Hell is like the slate dump.

Near the slate dump is another rocky hillside punctured by several small caves. We explored these caves for hours. The outside of the caves is lined with scrubby underbrush, sparse pine trees, and old trails that snake through the hillside. We must have walked miles and miles up and down the old trails, laughing and jumping over dead trees with trunks leaning on their sides.

Minden and Oak Hill youngsters love to prank each other around the caves and the slate dump. Geographically, the Oak Hill boys have the upper hand, as their home base is located up the hillside position above our town. In our minds, the Oak Hill boys were bigger and stronger, and had the high-ground advantage watching us come up the hill. Surprise attacks were out of the question. Oak Hill boys scared us with bow and arrows, and rocks rained down forcing our retreat.

One day the harmless play gets carried away and Brother Charles has a huge rock pushed down on him. Without time to protect himself, the enormous rock lands on his chest. Charles and my brothers are a bit scrawny, so the rock knocks him for a loop, falling backwards screaming in pain.

Sore, angry and slow moving, Charles gathers himself while his brothers and the other Minden boys, charge up the hill, hollering and yelling at the Oak Hill boys. The Oak Hill boys disappeared over the hill before the Minden gang can reach the top. We all know not to tell Mama or Daddy for fear they will forbid us to play at the caves. The line was drawn – we avoided the Oak Hill boys near the caves from that point forward.

Yards on the hill were rocky outcroppings jutting jaggedly from the earth. In the winter the snow melted in the direct sunlight; however, the soil was poor, leaving grass struggling to survive. We were born in a hill house, then moved to the hard road where grass was more abundant.

Minden youngsters playing. Houses are typical of ones on stilts.

Many houses have no bathroom plumbing; internal bathrooms were a luxury saved for the most privileged families. Most families, like ours, haul water from the kitchen to the big metal bathtub. Usually two or more of us washed in the same bath water before the tub was emptied. Toilets were in the outhouse.

Mama and her friends constantly talked of how windy it is in these stilted houses teetering perilously on the hillside, the mountain wind in a squealing barrel roll down to our hollow. You've never been as cold as it is on the mountain with naked trees and a whistling wind. The wind picks up anything not nailed down, even inside. Scattered rugs are lifted with ease with the wind coming through the floorboards in between the stilts.

In the summer, as it is now, this hillside is covered in dust and rock. Most of what is green on this hill are weeds and wildflowers mixed in with patches of grass which somehow survive in the rocky terrain. The wildflowers add a touch of color and beauty in the tough ground.

Scattered around our yard are the Forsythia bushes with their bright yellow blooms adding more color to our world. In the spring season, the mountains that enfold us hold Dogwood trees throughout the hillsides as they grow profusely. I think of our Sunday school class and the legend of the Dogwood Tree. The legend is that the Dogwood tree was the tree used for the cross that Jesus was nailed to during his crucifixion. Since the crucifixion, the Dogwood would never again grow strong enough to be used in such a cruel way.

When the wildflowers are in bloom, I pick them for Mama. With a smile, she places the wildflowers in a canning jar and sets it on the kitchen table. Gathering the wildflowers, a mixture of Buttercups and Dandelions and Daisies and whatever I can find, I run to hand them to mama as she sits on the front porch. Mama waves her hand and looks across our tiny yard and the hillside beyond which is speckled with my brothers and sisters and our friends as she says with maternal pride in her voice and the lazy drawl of the Appalachia, "All of y'all are wildflowers!" Her smile reflects pride as she takes the flowers.

One of the brothers hollers out, "Y'all ready to play tag?"

Another boy responds, "Why don't we fly June bugs? Does anyone have string?"

To fly a June bug beetle, first you must catch it and then attach a string loosely to one of its legs. This can be tricky. The string cannot be too tight, or it will break the bug's leg and if the string is too loose, the June bug will fly away. Sometimes the June bugs are scarce and difficult to find while other times there seems to be an endless supply. I can catch the June bug easily enough, but I need someone to tie the string while I hold it. We fly the June bugs like kites, letting the bug lead the way as we run behind it while it makes its buzzing sound. When we tire of them or they tire of us, we give the June bugs their freedom. Many of the June bugs lose a leg at this point, not intentionally, but it can be difficult removing the string.

This evening, we vote against flying June bugs and opt for hide and seek. The oldest coal camp kid is dubbed the seeker, and as he counts down with his eyes mostly closed, we quickly scatter for good hiding places out of view of his peripheral peeking.

After supper, when the twilight begins creeping in and the first stars begin to twinkle, we collect some of mom's old mason jars. We punch holes in the lids, stuff grass at the bottom of the jars, and search for lightening bugs under the dazzling night sky. Our area is full of lightening bugs in the summer and they are easy to catch. I always try to gather enough glowing bugs to glow the brightest. The lightening bugs or fireflies are magical as they light up. Before Mama calls us in for the evening, we open the jars and let the bugs fly off.

Summer days and evenings are filled with these endless yard games and countless friends. If we tire of one game, we go to another as Mama pops popcorn and passes out Kool-aide.

I begin thinking of us Minden coal camp kids as wildflowers, growing up in the hard-rocky ground of the hillsides, finding a place to grow in the rough terrain.

4

NEWSPAPER AD

Nine of us live in a five-room house rented to Dad by the New River & Pocahontas Coal Company. It is tough to financially support nine people in a family. It is even tougher when two of them have medical issues. As we hear many times in our life, "If y'all goin' have that many kids, y'all the ones that got to take care of them." Mama and Daddy did not expect any different. They are independent and self-sufficient and intend to stay that way.

We may not be living in this five-room house much longer. Mom saw an advertisement in the <u>Register, Beckley Post-Harold</u> newspaper that the coal company sold all its coal camp houses a few months earlier to the Blackburn-Patteson Realty Company. One of the owners of the real estate company, Okey L. Patteson, is a former Governor of West Virginia. Blackburn-Patteson is selling 300 coal camp houses, ranging from three to eight rooms, for $500 to $2,500 each.

Seeing the newspaper advertisement hit Mom like a ton of bricks. She knew about the inevitable fate of losing our home, word gets out fast in a small town. But seeing it in writing validated the rumor and quickly the gravity of the situation set in. Our house is being sold while we live in it. If someone buys it, we must move. She can no longer stay in denial. The illusion that everything is fine is shattered. Until now, Mom and Dad said little about the mines closing. The majority of the men have already been laid off and most mining operations have stopped. They just didn't talk about it.

The sadness on Mom's face and the stillness about her was unnerving, especially when we are accustomed to her excitable charm. "Things are changing," said Mama, resuming reading the newspaper without emotion. My siblings and I look at each other. We don't know what will change for us, but some changes are beginning to happen around us. Coal families are moving out with no place to go.

Our cupboards often run bare by pay day. We live pay check to pay check, and some families can't even make it until the next pay check. Those families borrow from the company store before pay days and the advance is taken out of the miner's pay check. When the mines shut down completely, the company store will also close. What will happen when Dad loses his job?

My sister Ann looks at Mom with inquisitive eyes, "Are we going to move?"

"Yes, eventually. We need a bigger house anyway," Mom says with simple honesty. I catch a gleam of tears gathering in Mom's eyes, so I rush off to play as a few tears drop to her cheeks.

Mom and Daddy don't discuss finances or problems in front of us, shielding us from those adult worries. Mama says, "You kids repeat what you hear," and "we don't air our dirty laundry." I don't know why she says this as everyone in town seems to know everything about everyone else anyway. Mom tells us not to worry. The simplicity of her statement gives us a sense of hope.

Coal camp kids have no interest in television except early in the morning or after darkness falls. When the work day is over, we watch the miners trudge home down the train tracks, shoulders bent over, covered in black coal dust with only the whites of their eyes showing. Sometimes they take showers at the bath house at the mines, so they come home clean. Even tired, they manage a smile or joke for us.

There are fewer miners walking down the track now. Many smiles show missing or tobacco stained teeth. The miners with their black soot covered faces and their slow imperfect grins represent strength and security to us.

We rush to meet Daddy with wild bursts of energy. Each of us want to be the first to reach him to win the cherished award of the leftover pie or cake from his lunch bucket. It's not just the award but the satisfaction of the win; we are all competitive. Daddy saves one of his packaged goodies each evening. We're not allowed to knock each other over or hit or push to reach him, but when it comes to the finish line, all seems fair to conquer that wrapped goodie which smells of the coal mine. I'm fast but seldom fast enough to get the cherished award. Even Sue, our oldest sister, races for the prize which surprises me because she is usually too mature for our childish silliness. She doesn't seem to think of it as silliness as she races to beat the brothers.

On weekends, Daddy takes the boys up to the bath house at the mines, so they can take showers. I always want to go but am not allowed. The boys come home telling us about their excursion and how they stop at the sand house and play in the sand before taking showers. Robert tells us the sand is always warm. Naturally, anything the boys do I want to do as well. Sue and Ann don't seem to care since girls can't take showers there. To pacify the girls, Daddy takes us occasionally on Sunday walks towards the mines and the sand house.

We are up early every day and have our meals together as a family. When school starts, our parents insist we go every day, although none of us try to skip school. I'm unsure if we like school or just the social life it brings.

Mama reminds us regularly that we need a good education, and things won't just land in our lap, we must work for it. There is never talk of the boys being miners. Daddy thinks the coal will be scarce when the boys get older.

I wonder how knowing our math tables inside out, spelling and diagraming sentences will get us a good job, but who am I to question. There is no privileged life for a coal camp kid. We don't travel to see the world beyond the hills. We are not surrounded by highly educated community members. We do not have access to emerging technologies, nor exposed to the arts. If Math and English will get us to an easier life, why not.

Deep in our thoughts are the occasional questions what and where will we go once Daddy loses his job. Other than the mines closing, there are no problems as far as we young ones are concerned except for our sister Ann who has a heart condition, or if one boy gets a larger slice of pie than the other which can cause an outright war.

Except trips with Mama to Oak Hill or to Charleston when Aunt Edie drives Mama and Ann to the doctor, I have not been out of Minden. In school, we read about different places and we see cities on the television, but none of it seems real.

The television breeds fear of atomic bomb attacks from the Russians. This seems a faded worry for us Minden folks compared to losing our jobs and homes. We contemplate what we will do if there is an atomic bomb attack, but no one in our town can afford to build a bomb shelter. No one has basements. We discuss going to the caves but being practical we know that will not save us.

For our sister Ann, she just wants a normal childhood without being treated differently. She wants a life full of promises, not fears. She doesn't want people to know she has a problem with her heart. Ann almost died when she was five. She had rheumatic fever which damaged her aortic value and enlarged her heart. She spent most of the year in and out of hospitals in West Virginia and Virginia. There were financial problems trying to get Ann admitted to a hospital that could care for her. The hospital in West Virginia was not equipped. Dad's insurance did not cover taking her to another hospital.

Mommy, who was sick from worry, cried a lot and was fussy, compounded by her erratic diabetes, leaving her sick as well. Mom and the doctor contacted every agency they knew to get help for Ann. Mom said that it doesn't seem right a child can't get medical help needed to keep her alive.

Finally, the program Crippled Children comes to our aid getting Ann admitted to a hospital in Richmond, Virginia where they specialize in heart issues like Ann's. Ann never fully recovered but was well enough to come home. The worry stays there waiting, leaving Mama and Daddy with a constant fear for her. Daddy says that you can't live in fear because it can eat away at you. He and Mama say we should be grateful for what we have.

We all have an unspoken admiration for Ann's strength and courage. She never complains and laughs and jokes with a sense of humor envied by others. She remains thin with a pretty face and dark curly hair like Mama. Boys always seem to be hanging around her.

Charles, Squeaky, John and Robert Crone in
Minden. Picture courtesy of Scott Crone.

Our brothers spare Ann their friendly physical heckling with their knuckle sandwiches, rubber band sling shots, spit balls and pink bellies. Our sister Sue doesn't indulge our brothers' pranks which doesn't make it fun for them. So, that leaves me. Unfortunately, I am not pardoned from the brothers' escapades. I am often a prime target when they tire of each other, unless I can move quickly and strategically out of their way. I have learned to fight, not like a boy but as a girl, kicking, scratching, and pulling hair to win the battle with no mercy. My brothers have been taught not to hit a girl, so I do have that to my advantage. Crying is not beneath me as a last resort.

We are usually quiet when adults are around. We have learned to be observant and respectful, speaking only when spoken to. Back talk is not acceptable. We call everyone by Mr. or Mrs. and respond with, "Yes or no sir." Since we spend more time listening than speaking to adults, we notice what they say and do. Town people are also fearful of what will become of them when the mine closes, so we are not alone.

Last week a neighbor came to the house wielding a bottle of whiskey looking scared and discombobulated. Mama, with her compassionate heart, sensed the neighbor's uneasiness, and shuffled us kids outside to play in the yard. Neither Mama nor Daddy drinks whiskey, but they don't want to be rude to the neighbor. Both are surprised by the neighbor. It's strange that Mama allowed the whiskey to stay, when our Uncle Bill stops by to talk, he sometimes attempts to bring a bottle of whiskey, too. Mom tells him right up front, "You can't be drinking whiskey in the house with all the youngsters, Bill."

Unlike Daddy, Uncle Bill has a loud voice and laughs and jokes easily assuring Mama he has no such thing, but as soon as Mom turns away, he pulls out the bottle and takes a swig. Daddy tells him he best put the bottle away before Lizzy sees it.

None of us tell on Uncle Bill but Mom keeps a watchful eye on him. One time she caught him red-handed. She promptly confiscated his bottle and warns that it may be poured down the sink. Uncle Bill just laughs and collects his bottle when he leaves.

Uncle Bill and his family moved out of Minden already. After he lost his job in the mine, he went to Indiana to work, moving his family there. Daddy is sad his brother moved so far away. Now he has no brothers in the area.

"I wonder what Mom will do with our neighbor's whiskey?" I ask. "I don't think our neighbor will laugh if Mom takes her bottle."

No one answers me. I don't know whose idea it was, but we decided to take turns sitting under the open kitchen window listening in on the adult conversation. The brothers are confident the eaves dropping will be exciting and at the very least will satisfy our curiosity knowing Mom and Dad will never tell us what is said.

"What do y'all reckon she wants?" I ask. Ann shushes me as we all cluster together near the window.

The boys take turns, one getting on his hands and knees and another sitting on his back allowing a closer proximity to the window. The remainder of us stoop and sit on our haunches anticipating an easy and fast escape, if needed. I'm unsure why the boys needed to get on each other's backs as we girls sitting under the window can hear just fine.

The boys strain their necks to hear and pass the information quietly to the rest of us. They must spy cautiously because Mama has eyes in the back of her head. Our neighbor seems to be grasping for words. Listening to the conversation through the open window, the best we can figure is that she is worried about what is going to happen now that the mines are shutting down. Her husband lost his job.

The neighbor's husband is a burly man with a barrel chest and a deep and loud voice boasting a heavy accent. I'm happy the husband didn't come to our house; he easily intimidates me but I'm generally shy and easily unsettled by men with loud and humorless voices. To me, he always looks "fit to spit nails" and I don't want the nails flying at me. Now, from what his wife says, he is frightened. I try to envision him frightened, but I cannot.

As we squat on the sparse grass under the window there is unexpectedly an outpour of emotion, our neighbor begins to sob. We can all hear her. Outpours of emotion are seldom seen here.

"I wonder if she had too much whiskey?" I ask.

Ann tells me, "Shoo, you can't talk, Sissy. She might hear us."

The neighbor cries out that there is no work to be found. She continues wailing that they have no family to go to and no way to feed their youngsters. Mom tries to console her as Daddy remains quiet.

I whisper, "We don't have any place to go either." Ann lifts her finger to her mouth to shush me again.

The neighbor tells Mama, "Look what happened to Clara's boy." *(Name was changed to protect family.)*

Daddy now speaks up, "People do crazy things when they get desperate but there's no cause for stealing. His Mama taught him better than that."

We know they are talking about the older boy up the road who robbed and shot someone a month ago. Sue read it in the newspaper and asked Mom about it. His Mama goes to our church.

Mom says, "His Mama is sick about it. She'd give you her shirt off her back and now her boy is stealing." Mama tells us, "Don't go talking about it." So, we don't.

Now the neighbor is talking about another woman named Maggie who lives nearby. *(Name changed to protect family.)* Our neighbor is upset that Maggie has a red light in her window late some nights. I've seen the red light and I asked Mama why they have a red light when Christmas is over, but Mama would only say, "I don't know" to keep its true meaning hidden.

Mama responds to our neighbor, "She's trying to put food on the table for her kids, I don't say it's right."

Our neighbor goes right on talking about Ralph Burgess having found a job out of state and no sooner did he start working, he dropped dead. We know about Mr. Burgess too since he and his wife were our parent's friends and went to our church. Ralph Burgess was born and raised in Conchu and the Minden area. His funeral was a couple months ago.

Purky, our rowdy and ornery neighbor boy, sees us crouched under the window. Purky is the type of boy who will pick a fight with anyone and I've seen him throw rocks at other boys. He always comes over to play, never fighting with us though. I'm not sure why he likes joining in our play since our brothers are not as ornery as he is, and Mama doesn't allow them to rough house. Mama's says he's really a good boy, just a bit rowdy.

Purky's curiosity has gotten the best of him as he stares perplexed and hollers out to us. Robert, who is taking his turn as the spy sitting on top of a brother's back, is startled and jerks up allowing Mama to see him. Annoyed, she motions for him to move away from the window.

Robert is one of those boys who continuously gets caught doing something he should not be doing. Well, come to think of it, Johnny does too. In Robert's hast to move, he falls off Charles's back and both go tumbling to the ground with Robert plunging backwards head first, feet flying in the air. We all collapse in the yard, legs entangled on the grass, covering our mouths trying to quieten our giggles. All we can do now is make a fast dash for the side yard by the honeysuckle bushes.

Purky with his curiosity piqued, jabs a finger in Ann's side as he calls out, "What are y'all doing? Who's in your house?" Ann ignores him at first but knowing his persistence, she puts her finger to her lips signaling him to be quiet. Reaching the side fence and the honeysuckles, I feel we are safe.

I suppose it is unfair and I would never admit it to my brothers, but I know Ann and I will be spared much of the grief. Ann is seldom reprimanded, and since I am the baby at the end of the pecking order, Mom and Dad often tire out before getting to me. They can only fuss so much, and they start with the boys first, but they are usually the ones that deserve to be scolded anyway.

Confident that we escaped, I look up to see George Crouch and Henry Dixon, our miner neighbors standing in their yards watching us.

I grab Ann's arm and say, "Look over yonder!" Ann turns to look across the street. Purky is not the only inquisitive mind around.

Still wondering what the red light is for, I wait until the boys join us then I ask the group. Purky responds, "She entertains men. The red light means she is available." Ann gives Purky a stern look as she shakes her head in disappointment. The boys smirk devilishly.

"How does she entertain them?" I ask. When no one answers, I quickly blurt out, "Does she give them whiskey?"

The boys smile and chuckle as Ann answers, "Maybe."

Charles, trying to change the conversation, calls out, "Who wants to shoot marbles?"

Charles is the marble champion in our little community. Johnny is good, too. There are official marble championship games in Minden. Men shoot marbles by the company store, and the brothers often shoot with them. I didn't think grown men play marbles, but in Minden it's a big deal.

"Can we play?" I call out. I don't play as well as Charles and Johnny, but I have my favorite cat eye marbles stashed in a secret place. The boys let me play on occasion. I usually lose, but the boys always return some marbles to me. Ann sometimes plays and she and I both only like the cat eyes. We girls can't flick the marble as hard or as accurate as the boys can, but we can outplay them any day with jacks.

"Charles," Robert says, "if you go in the house now to get your marbles Mom will fuss at you." Charles decides to wait for the neighbor to leave.

I call out, "We can play hopscotch." On to the next game we go. Not much else can we do. The neighbor's breakdown may take a while.

5

THE FLOOD OF 1956

Friday, July 27, 1956. The rains have been falling since yesterday. Streaks of lightning flash through the sky and thunder rocks our town, as the first electrical storm hits about 5:00 A.M. The storm releases a torrent of wind and rain.

In the predawn hours, the cracking of the thunder have me jumping up in bed frightened. The room is too hot and sticky. Our windows are normally left open at night to let in the cooler evening air, but someone shut our bedroom window during the night.

We have a couple fans in the house that circulate air on sultry summer days, but I don't know if they are running. It is stifling hot in our bedroom with the window shut. My pajamas are sticking to me.

The rain is pounding on the roof top and banging against the window in hard, rapid patters. It is not the soft gentle rain that is relaxing, but the type that people say God and the Devil are fighting using the lightning and thunder.

A bolt of lightning flashes by the window, illuminating the window and waking me fully. A gust of wind rattles our window panes making the curtains flutter. My body shudders, lightning is unsettling.

I share a bedroom with my two older sisters Sue and Ann, with me in the middle of our rod iron double bed often getting squashed and sandwiched between the two. Sue and Ann toss a bit this morning, but they appear to be asleep.

In addition to the familiar creaks of the house, I hear raised voices coming from the boys' bedroom. I quietly slip out of bed running barefoot across the linoleum floor, dashing to our kitchen in hopes to make it there before the lightning strikes again.

Our small kitchen is bright and cheerful and often smells of fresh baked goodies. The walls are covered in a sunny wallpaper pattern with various fruits colorfully displayed. Daddy, with the help from my brothers Squeaky and Charles, just laid the new linoleum on the floor last week, so the floor is still glossy because the wax has not yet dulled. Someone is always in the kitchen. I smell the aromas of coffee brewing and bacon frying, knowing Mommy and Daddy are there.

Mom's back faces me as she leans toward the kitchen stove with her dark hair, soft and shiny, curled loosely around her face. The habitual bobby pins she uses holds the hair from her eyes. Her hair is nearly black and there are only a few strains of gray streaming through. She jokes often telling us that we are giving her a head full of gray hair. She wears a cotton housedress this morning as she fries bacon in the old cast iron skillet.

Mom and Dad are creatures of routine. They eat the same thing for breakfast every morning: coffee, bacon, eggs and biscuits with jelly. This morning is no different. Daddy says that he doesn't have much, but he will always have lots of food on the table for his family. This family of nine eats a lot, especially the boys. Mom can't understand how the boys stay so scrawny when they eat so much.

On the few remaining days before pay day, the food becomes "bare pickings" which means spam or bologna for dinner. For the life of me, I cannot stomach spam no matter how Mama fixes it, but we always have lots of fresh vegetables in the summer which I love. We know pay day will again bring our favorites.

Mom is excitable and talkative and enjoys socializing. She loves and adores her Mama and her sisters who all used to live in Minden, but none of them live here now. Daddy says our Mom "wears her emotions on her sleeves."

Dad is a soft-spoken man with an easy-going temperament, a gentle man with lots of patience which seems to come easily to him. A short man compared to his brother Bill, Daddy has dark black hair, eyes green with speckles of brown with black coal dust that is embedded around the crevices of his eyes regardless how much he washes them. He always has a tidy appearance. He is not a big frame man, but his body is tough as a rock from the years of mining coal. Daddy still stands straight unlike many older miners who stand with shoulders slouched from the years of mining.

We don't hear our Daddy use foul language nor does he allow the boys to cuss although Mama does on occasion. Mom tells the boys she will wash their mouths out with soap if they use foul language.

Daddy doesn't complain about anything or anyone unless the person is lazy. He just shakes his head and says, "He's no count, he's too sorry to work," and the discussion of the person is dismissed with no other comments. I do not want to be lazy although my brothers say that I never do chores. I do, they just don't notice. It seems to me that if people don't want to notice something, they just tend to ignore it.

I hear Daddy talking about the rain this morning, he says that the heavy rain can be problems for the mines if it floods. Miners often work in a little water, but flooding is different.

As usual, Daddy is drinking a cup of coffee diluted with sugar and evaporated milk. His coffee is the color of oatmeal. His hands are rough with callouses and have short well-kept nails to keep the coal dust from settling under them, but the soot finds its way into any crack it can find.

Although Daddy is tough, his hands shake with each drink he takes. It's disconcerting to me that he is so tough, but his hands shake. He uses a saucer with his coffee cup picking both up at the same time, with part of the coffee ending up in the saucer every time. We say nothing about his shaking, but we wonder why. My older siblings say it is from the strenuous physical work he does. None of my brothers or their friends have a desire to work underground. Daddy doesn't want them to be miners either.

In the pre-dawn hours, I stand watching at the kitchen door, Dad reaches for his package of Beechnut chewing tobacco to put in his pocket. He is not a smoker; many miners chew tobacco instead of smoking. Daddy says chewing wads of tobacco helps keep the coal dust out of his throat. Even though he doesn't smoke, he has the miner's cough. Mama says it is from all the coal dust inhaled underground. Their lungs are probably covered in coal dust and soot, just like the outside of their bodies.

Anyone living around coal mines and coal towns knows that soot and dust finds its way into every nook and cranny. No wonder Daddy and his miner friends cough.

We don't know it now, but Daddy will be one of many miners who develop Black Lung.

Mom has eyes in the back of her head. She doesn't turn around but just asks me what I am doing up so early. I tell her the lightning and thunder scared me, as I wonder how she knows it is me and not one of the boys.

"Go back to bed, Sissy," she says. "It's too early to be up. The storm will be over soon, and I have to get your Daddy off to work," she mutters. "I have to go to the hospital this morning," she continues saying as she turns to me with a chin and nose a bit pointed inherited from her Hungarian parents. I inherited some of the same facial features. My brothers tell me I have gypsy features but ironically a couple of them have them, too. Looking like a gypsy seems more exciting than being a coal camp kid, so I don't mind. But, daddy tells me I look like his mama and have some of the German and Irish and English blood, so I don't know who I look like.

Our maternal grandparents moved here from Hungary. Hungarian genes are very strong in physical appearance; I unsuccessfully try to hold my chin in but give up accepting my Vegh genes. I truly don't like the sharp and bold features, but I can't cut off my nose and chin.

*"Apa" Grandpa and Grandma Andrew and Fanny
Grandetti Vegh settle in Minden in 1910. Apa was a coal
miner in Minden as were his sons Andy and John.*

To soften my appearance, I tell my brothers that it gives me a foreign look and I am proud of it. I learned early that if I act as if my brothers don't bother me they will get bored and find another victim. If the boys aren't picking on each other or me in some fashion, I worry something is wrong just like Mama worries if it gets too quiet.

Today, Mom must go to the hospital for her doctor and lab appointment. She is diabetic and has been since I was born. She catches a bus in Oak Hill where we do our major shopping. Mama shops in Oak Hill more often than the company store. Daddy doesn't want to "owe his soul to the company store," he says. This is also where the hospital, the high school and the movie theater are located although I have never been to a movie. The boys sometimes go.

We have no car and even if we did, Mom never learned to drive. She is not looking forward to drudging out in the downpour of unrelenting rain which does not appear to be stopping anytime soon. Mama usually returns home by bus unless she buys lots of groceries and catches a taxi home.

It is a constant struggle for Mom to stick to her diet, she has a weakness for sweets that is difficult to resist. "Sugar is addictive," she says as she tries to abstain from eating the baked goods she prepares for us. Temptation whispers beckoning us all in some form.

Mom unconsciously ruffles my sleep tangled hair and repeats her order for me to go to bed. "No pouting," she says as she looks at my lower lip.

"I'm not pouting," as I pull my lower lip back in. "Will you bring me back some paper dolls from town?" We consider Oak Hill as town.

Mama answers, "Yes, I will."

"Some fingernail polish, too for me and Ann?" I ask.

Mama responds, "Yes, if you go back to bed." So, I turn and shuffle back to the bedroom. I need to go to the toilet, but I don't want to go outside in the pouring rain, so I decide to hold it for as long as I can. Our toilet is in an outhouse. We are not fortunate enough to have an indoor bathroom. Coal camp houses were built cheaply with little to no frills. Since the coal company knows they are closing the mines, repairs to the homes are neglected, not that they did much repairing before that anyway.

Sluggishly I crawl across Ann's willowy frame to get in bed, activating a squeaky bedspring. I reach for a corner of one of the pillows to lay my head down. I know it won't last long, I wake most mornings with my head in between the two pillows. Our sheets are well worn, unmatched and practically thread bare but they are clean. On our bed is a handcrafted quilt that mama made from scrap material. We have a pink pastel chenille bedspread with a floral design that covers our bed during the day giving the bedroom a feminine touch. The floral wallpaper on the walls adds color and comfort. Our bedroom is kept tidy and clean even though three of us share it.

Mommy and Daddy loathe disorder and Mom preaches if things aren't clean one of us will get sick, and then everyone will be sick. Our home is ruthlessly clean with little clutter except for games, puzzles and comic books. There are no dirty dishes to be found in the sink or dirty clothes lying around. Our mismatched dishes are washed, and the kitchen is cleaned, swept and mopped daily. The little chores are almost effortless since we do them regularly. Without disciplined order our home could be a disaster with nine people in such small quarters. Our home never looks messy.

We possess no heirloom treasures, no china, no silver and no crystal. Squeaky says when he goes off to the Army, which he plans to do after school, he's going to buy Mama some china dishes for special occasions.

Ann wakes up and asks why I'm awake so early. Sue rolls over and tells us both to go back to sleep. The rain continues to pound and splash on our roof top. I lay quietly, listening to the rain from the comfort and security of our bed, as the sky glows briefly from the flash of lighting.

I drift back asleep until another loud thunder rumbles again. I hear the boys talking and laughing. Their bedroom is next to ours and the walls are thin. My brothers have a job delivering newspapers, so they are up early most days.

The constant patter of falling rain reminds me I need to pee. Rain or no rain, I can't wait any longer. I scramble out of bed and back to the kitchen.

Mom pulls back the curly strands of hair that escaped her bobby pins as she looks my way. I quickly tell her before she has time to speak, "I have to pee!" as I uncross my legs and run outside to the toilet grabbing a jacket to throw over my head.

As I swing open the screen door, mom yells out, "Don't slam the door."

We know all our neighbors, so we feel safe outside even in the dark. The doors to our house are not locked until everyone goes to bed and then windows are open. Our dog, Boy, barks if anyone comes near. As I run outside, the smarting wind and rain sweeps over my body. I am

36

no longer hot and sweating but have rain water running down my arms and legs, struggling to hold the jacket over my head.

Outhouses are placed behind the houses as far back as the small yards allow. The outhouse is a small shed structure. It has no lights, no windows, no heat and no running water. It is painted white with black trim same as all the houses. When the sky is dark with few stars, the inside of the outhouse is pitch black. We put the porch light on and keep the outhouse door open, so we can see. The toilet is a seat with an opening in the middle centered above a pit. It smells in the summer and is cold in the winter. Water lines are installed in the houses to provide running water but there are no sewer lines and no sewer tanks for bathrooms in most of the houses.

We are raised to be grateful for what we have, but I can't help hating the toilet, and find it difficult to be grateful for it. Whining and complaining will not change our circumstances, so as much as we dislike it, we accept it for what it is now but not what it will be. We look forward to the day we have an indoor bathroom.

A woman living near Scrapper's Corner in Minden nearly fell into an old toilet hole recently. The outhouse itself had been moved to a newly dug hole, but the old hole had not yet been filled in with dirt. The woman forgot about the open hole, and nearly fell in. I don't know how she held on. She was rescued just in the nick of time. The mining company eventually filled the old toilet hole with dirt. The thought of falling into a toilet hole is too revulsive to even ponder.

During Halloween, outhouse toilets can often be found turned over. Some of the boys consider it a Halloween trick, especially for those who are not generous with candy. Fortunately, to my knowledge, no one was using a toilet at the time it was overturned.

My brothers Squeaky, Charles, Robert and Johnny have gotten out of bed and are standing in the kitchen. Squeaky is a nickname that stuck with Reginald from the early days when Uncle Andy said he constantly made sounds like squeaking noises. He is named after Daddy, but no one calls Squeaky by his real name. Squeaky started delivering newspapers at 11 years old and now the other boys help, too.

I stand in the enclosed porch that serves as an addition to our kitchen as I attempt to dry off my drenched arms and legs. I am now wide awake with no desire to go back to bed. I wonder how anyone can sleep with all these booming sounds and flashing lights across the sky.

Arbuckle Creek is usually a small stream of water, but it will not be today. The water is rapidly rising, which we are fearful of living close to the creek. At least, we do not border the creek as do many of the houses. The shallow creek is narrow often overflowing during heavy spurts of rain. The yards of the houses sitting closest to the creek or those with low elevation often flood. Water runs off the hills too, so the flood waters come quickly. The creek water is dirty and brown with mine soot and whatever else may run into it, leaving what it touches stained and needing disinfecting.

Mom finishes packing Daddy's lunch putting the sandwiches and packaged cakes in the top of the bucket, adds water to the bottom portion of the bucket and sets the tall metal lunch pail on the table facing me. I look at the lunch pail and immediately think of what the boys recently told me. They said miners carry metal lunch pails, so the rats and mice can't eat their lunch. I didn't believe them, thinking they just want to watch me gasp in horror which they love doing. With both fears of the storm and the rats bouncing around in my head, I ask Daddy, "Is it true there are rats in the mines and they try to take your lunch?"

Daddy is a man of few words so when he talks, we listen. He glances at the boys who continue to stand around the kitchen with wide eyes, and then looks at me as he slowly nods his head up and down to tell me it is true. Chills run through my body, thinking of rats scurrying around. Rats are so disgusting. I have seen a river rat or mine rat as they are called. They are not little mice that some people think are cute, but the big ugly rodents.

Miners have more to fear than rats, even big disgusting ones. Every day the miners face the damp, dark underground, knowing the rooftop can cave in, or slate can fall on them burying them alive. Tunnels flood and methane gas can explode igniting fires.

Grandpa Vegh lost his toes on one foot from a mine accident and Daddy had slate fall on him a couple times injuring his arm and hand. Uncle Jake, Daddy's brother, died a few years ago from a mining accident in the Minden mine when a machine malfunctioned, breaking his neck.

Stalling so I don't have to go back to bed, I ask questions that dance and pop around in my mind like the bacon jumping and sizzling in the iron skillet. I blare out, "Do the rats scare you?" "Do they crawl on you?" "Do they bite?" I begin squealing in disgust, not waiting for answers.

Dad snickers. He is not one with a loud boisterous laugh. I think he knows I am stalling so he goes along with me. Through a slow grin he says, "They don't bother us, but they do try to carry our lunches away. They can't get in the metal lunch buckets. Of course, if you are sleeping, they might take a bite of you instead."

Robert quickly bursts out, "I told you, Sissy, I told you, but you wouldn't believe me!" Charles and Johnny stand beside him shaking their heads up and down in agreement. The oldest child, Squeaky slowly shakes his head back and forth, annoyed by all of us, and lets out a resounding sigh.

"It's not my fault I didn't believe you," I reply. "It's their fault," as I point at Charles and Johnny.

"Why is it our fault?" Charles pipes. Lanky thin Johnny peers out at me with bright blue, long lashed eyes and a freckled face, and then looks towards his brothers, conflicting on who to support, not wanting to take sides. People say that a girl would kill for Johnny's eyes.

"They tell me not to believe a word you say, Robert, cause you're always tellin' a story," as I look up with what I think is my best angelic charm laced with a slash of hurt. "I don't know who to believe," which truly I don't.

Robert squints narrow-eyed at his brothers with a bruised ego as if his brothers betrayed him. I feel a small wave of relief that the betrayal is being directed from me to them. Everyone suddenly has something to say all at the same time as feelings intensify and mixed voices swell throughout the kitchen.

Robert, a small frame boy with an olive complexion, welcoming smile, and a mop of dark curly hair like Mom, loves to weave a story or a tall tale. Everyone says not to believe Robert. He paints his stories with such vitality and sincerity that it is difficult not to believe him. It's a game to him. Mom says Robert should be a salesman or a politician.

Johnny, the easy-going brother who everyone gets along with, is never the instigator but will join in with the others out of brotherly obligation. He often supports Robert's stories which gives them even more credence. Robert even has our older brother Charles believing his stories which irritates Charles that he is deceived when he finds out the stories are untrue.

Razzing each other is the way the brothers show affection. Their squabbles are seldom true squabbles. I think my brothers are the wittiest creatures whether I can believe them or not.

Mom turns to look at us as she frowns and asks, "Why is everyone talking at the same time about rats at the kitchen table?" She then shakes her index finger, a habit she picked up when she fusses at us. We know she is serious if she shakes her index finger with no smile on her face. This morning she is smiling so we know she is not truly upset.

No one responds verbally, but in unison we collectively shrug our shoulders. One of the boys bursts out with, "Sissy started it."

"Mommy, I didn't start it. They did," I quickly reply.

Mama tells us all to stop talking.

Daddy's lips are curved into a smile as he enjoys the richness of the morning. He grabs his lunch bucket and gives Mom a kiss and a hug. Except for the very young or very old, hugs are not overly abundant in our home. I seldom see people greeting others with a hug. An arm across the shoulder or a pat on an arm or hand is equivalent to a hug. But, then again, emotions are seldom displayed openly whether it be sadness or happiness. Emotions are kept subdued and bottled inside.

Daddy steps out of the kitchen door, the screen door squeaks as he leaves us with an order, "You kids watch out for your Mom," as he always tells us. Daddy always worries about Mom. Even after being married 18 years, Daddy is sweet on Mom.

Mama asks the boys, "Do you want cream of wheat or oats for breakfast? I don't have time to fix anything else this morning."

Outside, our dog, Boy, hears Daddy and runs out of his dog house regardless of the rain, expecting a treat and a pat as reward for sitting dutifully. Boy is happy with the simple pleasures. Daddy pats him on the head, scratches his ear, and gives him a piece of bacon and biscuit saved from breakfast.

Squeaky found Boy deserted one morning while he was delivering newspapers. Boy was a skinny puppy, and Mommy and Daddy agreed he could be part of the family. Squeaky says Boy is his dog, but the other brothers declare him everyone's dog, but in my opinion Boy has a special love for Daddy.

We know Daddy will meet up with other miners like George Crouch, Henry Dixon, Nelson Webb, Andy Wooten or my Uncle John Vegh while they walk up the track to the mine. Uncle Andy Vegh, a Fire Boss, continues to work at the mine but he moved to Oak Hill recently.

At the height of coal mining operations, over 600 miners worked in Minden, but recently only 62 miners completed the U.S. Bureau of Mines accident-prevention course for the Minden mine, all of whom are listed in an article published in the local newspaper, the <u>Post-Herald and Register</u> in Beckley. Dad was among those in attendance. The 10-week course covered all types of mining accidents.

The men who attended this training are:

> *Wallace W. Gwinn, superintendent; George H. Crouch, loader and local union president; Hassel Andy Adams, car cleaner; John Alley, trackman; Columbus C. Barrett, loader; James Bates, loader; Theodore Bednarsky, bratticeman; Nat Blanks, brakeman; Carl David Blevins, brakeman; Theron W. Bowyer, welder; Everett Guy Burgess, wireman; E.D. Barnett, shuttlecar operator; Elmer Caldwell, truck driver; Albert Ray Canterbury, laborer; Ernest M. Chandler, foreman; Archie Corbett, loader; Russell W. Cox, loader; Buster R. Crone, slateman; Charles W. Crouch, timberman; Robert Crouch, lampman; Gordon Leon Dempsey, fire boss; Henry Dixon, trackman; William*

John Douglas, loader; Dave Duncan, loader; Wilbur F. Eigenbrod, safety inspector; Sam Franco, loader; W.D. Goins, bonder; Earl Hall, loader; Kelly Hague, brakeman; John Hurst, motorman; John Hawkins, trackman; Fred Wilson Huddleston, repairman; Charles H. Leach, electrician; Albert Lewis, loader; Basil H. Light, loader; Frank Lokant, loader; C.D. McClaskey, fire boss; William P. McGrady, foreman; Castro Malines, loader; Ulyssas A. Mosby, loader; Frank Munoz, motorman; Willard C. Neely, trackman; William Herman Neuse, loader; Gary Osborne, laborer; John Price, foreman; Raymond J. Rakes, trackman; Leonard Rhodes, loader; Emory Richman, machine operator; Henry Samuels, foreman; Christopher Straddling, laborer; Gines Tabondela, loader; Glenroy O. Toles, pipeman; Antonio Tolinsky, timberman; George Kinner Tracy, pipeman, Andrew J. Vegh, Jr., fire boss; William Waters, loader: John Watson, loader; Nelson E. Webb, loader and Andy Wooten, fire boss.

Most miners were laid off last year. We know Andy Wooten, also a Fire Boss, will be leaving the mines soon. He found a job teaching school. Coal mining pays more money than teaching, but Mr. Wooten will at least have a reliable and respectable job while his fellow ex-miners are still job searching.

We watch out the window as Daddy crosses the road and his steps take on a steadfast pace trudging through the rain. On both sides of this narrow road riddled with potholes are rows of houses running parallel with the road. Roads in town are mostly dirt or red dog, named Duncan Hill, Dog Holler and Daisy Hill where the elementary school is located. Although the houses and hills have numbers, there are no mailing addresses, as mail is delivered to the central post office, not door-to-door. If you tell someone where you live, you say the hill number, who lives near you or a physical location in town such as the company store or the post office. We live near Scrapper's Corner on the hard road.

Scrapper's Corner acquired its name because of the many fights and tussles that occur there. Bigger boys hang out at that corner. When boys outside of town try to enter, the Scrapper's Corner boys throw rocks or verbally and physically attack with "rocks and fists flying." I'm unsure how or when it started, but it deteriorated to the point that Scrapper's Corner boys even picked on other Minden boys passing by their territory. Bill Harmon, a boy who lives a few houses up from Scrappers Corner, told me that his Mama said he can thank his Uncle Frog for giving Scrapper's Corner its name. According to his mama, his uncle was one of the kids doing the fighting. Tussles became so well-known that the name Scrapper's Corner stuck.

Hearing about the fighting, Mom was so upset that she was ready to tangle with the tormentors herself if they didn't leave her boys alone. She went to the Justice of the Peace to complain as well as to the boys' families. Since our house is close, it is difficult to avoid Scrapper's Corner, but we go up the side of the hill or down the railroad track to avoid it. Eventually the Scrapper's Corner boys leave my brothers and their friends alone if they don't get too close. My brothers and their friends are not ones to back down from a fight. They will take their *lickins'* but since most of them are a bit scrawny and Mama is nearby to holler at the bigger boys, the big boys seem to lose interest in my brothers and their friends. Daddy says that if he had Mama coming after him when her dander is up, he would leave her youngsters alone, too.

The Minden mines are a short distance up the railroad track from our home. George and Helen Crouch live in the house which sits diagonally from ours. There is a rickety walking bridge that is behind he and his neighbor Henry Dixon's houses and which crosses over Arbuckle Creek. Crossing the bridge, allows for a short cut to the mine down the railroad track and a short cut to Bates store.

I'm unsure who built the walking bridge. It's not a real bridge but a few boards put together to cross the narrow creek. The bridge is designed for one person to walk across at a time and it wobbles when you cross it. There are no handrails. I avoid crossing the bridge at the same time as my brothers since they like to jump up and down and make it wobble.

There are not many stores in Minden. There is the company store with the attached drug store and malt shop, the post office, the barber shop, the shoe repair shop, the doctor's office, several churches and a couple small stores. Most of these will be closing or have already closed. For the life of me, I can't understand why there is a shoe repair shop since most people can't afford expensive shoes to repair. It is hardly worth repairing inexpensive shoes.

There are no racial problems in our town as far as we are aware. We read in the newspaper about The Civil Rights Movement. Racism seems to be in the mainstream of life, but here everyone is treated equally albeit we live in separate parts of town. The African American families, who during this time are called "colored," live on the upper end of Minden along Old Minden Road near the coal mines and Oak Hill. The "white" folks live in the lower part of Minden. The upper end does not seem any better or worse than the lower section.

Mr. and Mrs. Bates are one of the few African American families that we know. They have a small store in the enclosed porch of their home. We walk to their store almost daily. On Sunday afternoons, we hike with Dad, sometimes up Old Minden Road by where Mr. Bates lives. Many of the men call out to Dad since they know him from the mines. He stops to talk as we wait patiently.

As in other parts of the country during these times, African Americans go to different schools and different churches, due partly to us living on opposite sides of town. In Minden, everyone goes to the same stores, the same doctor, catch the same bus and work together at the mines. The men all call each other by their first names and all the kids call adults by Mr. and Mrs. There is talk that soon we will all be going to the same schools, and nobody seems to care much.

Mr. Bates works with Daddy and our uncles at the mines and is happy we support his store. He and his wife are extremely friendly, laughing and talking with us when we go to their store. Rumor in town is that Mr. Bates sells moonshine. Our brothers are convinced that Mr. Bates stocks moonshine in his toilet. Bill Harmon told us that his cousins took some out of the toilet one night. The Bates' outhouse sits behind their home near the creek where the ground is softer.

My brothers and some of their friends attempted to dig underground to reach the inside of their outhouse hidden from behind. To their disgust, they dug into the useable portion of the outhouse. No moonshine was found---only a useable toilet. No one admitted who masterminded this disaster. The boys with flutters of panic in getting caught attempted to cover the tunnel and escaped undiscovered with only sweaty, rumpled clothes and stinky bodies as rewards of their efforts.

God smiled upon the boys that evening because if Mommy and Daddy knew they certainly wouldn't be smiling. The boys have refrained from further attempts to find the moonshine. At least until one of them can come up with a new scheme.

The storm with its torrential rain continues to rage and is at its worst from 8:30 until later morning. The miners are called out of the mine and sent home for fear of flooding and power loss. The railroad tracks are covered with water which runs down the track into the narrow creek and overflows into the yards bordering the creek.

About 9:00 A.M., there is an unusually loud crash heard over the thunder. We hear the noise at our house. It's unfamiliar. Perhaps lightning hit something? We see people rushing towards Scrapper's Corner in total disregard of the downpouring rain. Someone outside yells that the slate dump fell down the hill. We are not far from the slate dump but luckily our house does not sit directly below it as others do.

There is an exhilarating excitement brought on by this disaster - the chaotic activity was uncommon. Mouths fly open and eyes are wide as we too want to see. We can't imagine the nasty slate dump tumbling down with its tons of slate.

Daddy returns from the mine and will not allow us to see for ourselves. We must stay on our covered front porch. He warns us that we don't want to be under a slate slide. The slate dump is huge and there is much left that can still come tumbling down.

From the covered front porch our view is blocked by a small curve in the road just a couple houses away at Scrapper's Corner. The wind blows the rain against us, but no one retreats except to lean against the house wall. Daddy grabs a hat and walks up the road to see what all the commotion is about with orders for us to stay where we are.

Daddy finds to his astonishment a portion of the slate dump previously smoldering on the hillside, now covers the hard road. Not only did the black debris fall onto the road but also onto the home of Frank Krazenek and a vacant home next door. Mr. and Mrs. Krazenek heard the crash before seeing it and were able to quickly run out of their front door seconds before the slate debris covered their home.

Everyone is astonished that the Krazenek's were not injured or killed. It is a miracle.

Minden 1956 Flood. Picture courtesy of Minden Reunion 2005. Rocks and slate shown are from the slide.

Minden 1956 Flood. Picture courtesy of Minden Reunion 2005.

Several tons of rock, slate and mud poured through the five-room home. As the water, rock and slate flowed down the hill, neighbors estimate the water was 20 feet high or higher. A wall is torn loose, and mud, slate and sludge rests in the house about three feet deep. The sludge is up to the top of the house on one side.

Even with the flood waters rising, people continue to run past our house up the road to catch a glimpse of the fallen slate dump. Jack Garcia, a native of Spain and a retired coal miner who settled in Minden, heard and saw the slate slide. Mr. Garcia "thought the end of the world was coming" when it hit. All the trees are turned over by the weight of the slate, rocks and water crashing down. Mr. and Mrs. Garcia live just down the road where the slate dump collapsed, so he had a direct view. We live further down the road past the Garcia's.

We're anxious to scan the area but Daddy holds us back. Our curiosity is overwhelming. There are more people on the road than I've ever seen at one time. It's a social event now, our neighbors standing on porches talking with one another, seemingly unaware of the pounding rain and rising flood water.

Someone calls the National Guard unit in Oak Hill to quickly transport families from their homes out of the slide area to safer locations. The National Guard stays in Minden for some time after the rescue to prevent curiosity seekers from entering the destruction area. In addition to damaging homes, the slate, rock and mud fall onto Minden Road blocking traffic access in and out of town.

Some neighbors climb on roof tops to watch the flood in action. You do not desert your home unless you have no other choice. We have never experienced this much excitement and the tinge of fear that goes with it.

Shortly after the land slide, an electrical storm knocks the power and telephone lines out. It is nearly 9:30 A.M. and the rains keep coming. Water flows out of the creek bed onto nearby land. From our house, we watch the water rise.

Daddy instructs us to go through the house and pick up everything that is on the floor or low to the ground and place them on top of the iron rod beds and tables. We move quickly and quietly. Johnny grabs the comic books making sure they are tucked in safely on the beds, and I cover my beloved paper dolls and board games with a pillow. Ann and Sue grab what few pictures we possess and clothes that are in low dresser drawers and stack them on the beds already covered with other household items. Our worn sofa in the living room and our kitchen table are stacked high.

Our house has never been in such disarray, resembling a disaster itself with our worldly possessions piled on top of each other. It is astonishing to see our home in such disorder. Mama would not be happy if she was here.

Daddy loves the big standup console radio that sits in the living room. He listens to it every night, seeking the comfort and relaxation that music brings. He eyes the radio and the television, probably our most monetarily valuable items, but they are too big to move.

Daddy worries about Mom who is in Oak Hill for her doctor's appointment. He paces the floor and says little. He always gets quieter when he frets, which I find unsettling. I am grateful we don't live bordering the creek.

The road is closed. There is no power and the phone is not working. Mom should be finished with her appointment at the hospital by now. Her original plan was to walk from the hospital to the bus station to wait for the bus to Minden, but now it's anyone's guess. The bus can't enter the town since the road is closed.

Daddy knows Mommy has little money with her and she needs to eat on a regular basis so not to get sick. He makes his decision. He will walk to Oak Hill to find Mom. He's concerned about her with diabetes and knows she will be anxious and uneasy about our safety. He figures that he can walk over the hill behind the slate dump, bypass the fallen slate, and follow the old lumber road. Daddy tells Squeaky he is to walk with him, and Sue and Charles will oversee the house and the rest of us.

With concern on her face and a quiver in her voice, Sue calls out, "But, Daddy, what if our house floods? The creek is already overflowing. What do I do with the kids?"

Daddy assures Sue it will be fine. He tells her that if the flood waters come up to the house, she and Charles are to take the kids and Boy to the top of the hill behind our house, leaving everything else in the house. This hill is separate from the slate dump. He tells her we will be safe if we stay on our hill.

6

RESCUING MOM

Friday, July 27, 1956. Daddy walks through the house one more time, pausing in the kitchen with a distant stare in his eyes. He tells us a story of when he was a teenager. Most evenings our grandmother, his Mama, walked down the railroad track to visit her daughter who was married, living in Minden. Normally, my Daddy or one of his brothers met their Mama to walk her home after dark. When the rain fell quickly and unexpectedly, none of the boys wanted to go out in the downpour. They failed to escort her home. She arrived home drenched and disappointed.

He told us his Mama had been ill for a long time prior to that night. She had Typhoid and survived the illness when many others died, but ultimately it affected her heart. Being the oldest son, Daddy left school to work in the mine to help financially, telling himself once his Mama got better he would go back to school. Eventually she got better, and he returned to school which made her very proud.

The morning following the rainstorm, he tried to wake up his Mama before he left for school but was unable to. His Papa was at the coal mine working, so he ran the mile or so to alert the company doctor. He ran back to wait with his Mama for the doctor's arrival, which seemed to take forever. She died while they waited. The day his Mama died was the day Daddy lost confidence in the coal company doctors and he always remained skeptical of them.

Those memories stuck in his mind like a thorny spike. As he tells us the story, he sadly says, "You can't take back something you do or don't do."

"Your mama will always be there for you." He would never have the chance to walk his Mama home again and for that he was sorrowful.

He won't leave his Lizzy stranded in the rain today. He hollers out, "Squeaky, let's go get your Mommy." Squeaky looks like a younger and slimmer version of Daddy in a lot of ways. His hair, a blondish light chestnut color, isn't as dark as Dad's, and he has less muscle. Squeaky will be starting his senior year in high school. He has not completely grown into his adult body yet, but no doubt will be short like Daddy. Squeaky is a hard worker and everyone says he doesn't gripe about doing chores.

Dad pulls his Beechnut chewing tobacco out of his pocket, takes a wad from the bag and shoves it in his mouth heading out the door. Squeaking rushes to keep in step with him.

Sue says to us, "I wonder if going after Mommy will help Daddy, too?" None of us younger kids are sure what she means.

Dad's steps take on speed and intent as Squeaky hurries to keep up. Water is over their shoes.

We often put cardboard in our shoes to help keep our feet dry, especially in the winter. The water can seep through the soles of our inexpensive shoes making our feet wet and cold. Cardboard does help. Unfortunately, Squeaky didn't have time to cut out cardboard to put in his shoes today, but it wouldn't have mattered anyway.

In the meantime, after Mom's doctor appointment at the hospital, she visited with her sister, Margaret, who is a nurse at the hospital, before rushing off to G.C. Murphy to purchase the items she promised to bring home.

She pulls out a scribbled note of which comic books to purchase, along with paper dolls, fingernail polish and crossword puzzle books. Mama enjoys crossword puzzle books probably more than we do. She bumps into Marjie Zastawniak who works there. Marjie and Mommy have been friends since they were young girls, both born and raised in Minden and continue to live there.

Marjie tells Mama that she tried to call home to check on her boys and the telephones are out of service. Marjie's home sits on higher ground. She's unsure if she will be able to make it home later if the rains continue. Mama starts worrying about her own kids knowing our house rests on lower ground. She scurries to the bus station.

Mom tucks the bag of purchased items under her sweater trying to keep them dry as she walks to the bus station. The rain scarf has done little to protect her hair which is now in wet sassy curls choosing their own direction. The umbrella is blown inside out and is useless in the storm as the wind lashes and tugs at it.

The walk to the station seems much longer today, especially being drenching wet and anxious to get home. Her wet dress clings to her body and her shoes make squeaking noises with each step.

Finally, she jumps on the bus headed to Minden. She doesn't know about the slate dump land slide at the bottom of the hill in Minden. The bus moves slowly and when it reaches the top of Minden hill, they discover it is completely flooded. The bus driver announces that they will have to return to the station.

Unsure what to do, Mom makes the decision to get off the bus to make her way down Minden hill. After all, her kids may be home alone; her husband stuck at the mine. She quickly evaluates that she can wade through the water and contemplates the best direction.

The Oak Hill Transit Company, the local bus company for the surrounding area, has a garage at the top of the hill. The parked buses are filled by the water flowing in this area. Minden hill is not only flooded but rocks and debris cover the road as well, leaving the road impassable.

No stranger to this area, Mama carefully maneuvers around the debris. Uncertain what lies ahead, she gets more apprehensive with each step.

Thinking to herself, the mine is surely closed, so Buster should be at home. It would be much too dangerous to work in the mines today. As she agonizes over the rains, she wonders if the valley below is flooded, too. With each step, her slip-on shoes become heavier and more difficult to walk in, almost falling off her feet. The rocks and debris only worsen the situation. Each step is painful.

She walks cautiously, not wanting to misstep as the shoes offer no protection. No cars are coming up the hill, so she realizes if she falls, who knows when she will be discovered.

As minutes pass, through the rain she sees Buster and Squeaky walking towards her waving and yelling her name. Seeing them is sheer delight as she waves back and realizes her upper back and shoulders ache from tension.

Minden is not the only town suffering from the floods. In Oak Hill six feet of water is flowing over cars. Before this storm is over, there will be 100 families in West Virginia washed out of their homes.

Left at home to restlessly wait for Mom and Dad and Squeaky, Sue insists we don't step foot off the front porch. Sue has a quick and easy smile with a youthful softness, a quiet voice to go with the face, and curly sandy brown hair. Glasses give her an intellectual look, which fits her because she is our intellectual sibling with or without the glasses. Today she has a sternness about her that we seldom see. She grips her slender and delicate hands, and her eyes keep straying to the creek across the road. She pleads with the boys to not do any foolishness until Daddy gets back.

With dreams of being a reporter, Sue realizes what great news coverage this will be. She is excited and enthusiastically anticipates seeing the slate dump land slide and what it destroyed.

Sue is a member of the National Honor Society, the Press Club, the Log Staff, and the Acorn staff for the school yearbook. She says these will give her experience in writing. I can't imagine why anyone would write if they didn't have to, but Sue even writes poems for fun.

Sue is a rule follower so if Dad tells her to keep us at the house until he returns, she is bound and determined to do so even if she wants to go out herself. Daddy knows she is the right one for the job keeping watch over his clever boys who will attempt an escape.

Ann and I are no match for Sue's watchful eye, but I am confident that our brothers will be successful in their escape. They are not unruly boys, just a bit inquisitive, and when told to stay within a fence, they will straddle it every time to get what's on the other side.

Near the landslide live our friends, Rupert and Donny Chuyka, the Campbell boys, Harold Hewitt, the Harmon family, and Mrs. Sifers, who is one of Mom's friends. The thought that our friends can see the destruction and are part of the excitement is excruciatingly painful to the brothers. They squirm and run back and forth from one window to another, then to the front porch to gather whatever news they can discover from those passing by. We are itching to get off the porch.

Ann and I occupy Sue's attention, so the boys can run to Scrapper's Corner. They get a brief glimpse of the slide before running back to the porch acting as if they were there the whole time.

Someone nearby says that with all that black sludge and slate in the road and stacked on houses it "looks like a piece of Hell fell out of the sky." The brothers shake their head in agreement.

The big question on everyone's mind is why did the slate dump slide down after all these years? The coal company regularly hauls waste products from the mines to an area on the hilltop. This slate dump is huge and towers over part of town as it smokes and burns in places. It is higher than some of the hills surrounding us. As the discarded pieces of coal and slate burn and bake, they form a hard reddish and orange rock like brick. This rock is called red dog and is used to cover roads and pot holes. Many of the roads in the county are made of red dog or patched with red dog.

Recently, a road maintenance crew dug a gigantic hole in the slate dump to extract the red dog. Perhaps today's torrential rains filled the mammoth hole until a substantial portion of the slate dump slid down under the unruly weight of the rock and water. It did so in an explosive manner.

Finally, with no word from Dad, Mom, or Squeaky, we receive some good news. The power in Minden is restored by 11:00 A.M., but phone lines still do not work.

The sound of our front porch door opening has never sounded sweeter than when Mom, Dad and Squeaky appeared. The rain stops shortly after, and the floodwater begins to recede at 1:00 P.M.

By late afternoon, we are finally allowed to leave our porch to see the damage. The gobs of mud, slate and debris lay thick across the road, on houses, and covering yards. It is a sad sight compounding to the misery that has invaded our town recently. Our feelings of excitement to see the destruction turned immediately into sadness. The only thing to do is begin the clean-up.

Minden Flood 1956. Pictures taken after water begin subsiding.
Slate dump can be seen towering over the town on lower
right picture. Pictures courtesy of Jane Webb Terry.

We learned later that Paquita Ripoll, a childhood friend of Sue and Squeaky, had waited for her dad to come home from the mines when the floods began. The longer she waited the more anxious she became, so she decided to walk to the mines to find her dad. Paquita realized she could not go down in the mine but attempted to find him nonetheless.

Like all youngsters of Minden, she knew how to maneuver around the hills to avoid the flood areas. When she arrived at the mine entrance, her dad was coming out along with Mr. Crouch, an elder miner who had difficulty with his knees. Mr. Ripoll had stayed to help Mr. Crouch out of the mine; a miner will never leave his comrade in danger.

Seeing Paquita walking towards them, Mr. Ripoll was very upset as it is much too dangerous for her to be there. She could be electrocuted or washed away. All the same, Paquita was just happy to see her dad even if he was fussing at her.

The next day, the Union Hall in Minden connected to the two-room school house, serves as the headquarters for interviewing families affected by the floods. The interviews are conducted by representatives of the Red Cross, the Rev. Landrum who is Chairman and Mrs. Gladwell, who is Secretary of the Fayetteville Chapter of the Red Cross. Wallace Gwinn, the superintendent of New River & Pocahontas mine operation, also assists with the rehabilitation program.

Helen Crouch, wife of George Crouch, who lives across the road from us, works for Blackburn-Patteson Real Estate and is assigned to collect contributions to be distributed to families in Minden affected by the flood. George Crouch, the President of the United Mine Workers Local Union, helps too.

In the aftermath, people gather to share their stories, their grief, their encouragement and the miraculous feelings that no one was injured or killed.

*Clean up after the 1956 Minden Flood. Picture
courtesy of Minden Reunion 2005.*

Equipment is brought into Minden to remove the black slate spilled over the hillside and road. The water receded enough for the debris and slate and rocks to be removed. The land is left mud stained, with grass and flowers uprooted. Our little coal camp looks dismal and murky, everything the waters touched must be cleaned and disinfected.

Machinery is brought in to widen Arbuckle Creek in the event of future floods. Portions of the muddy earth along the creek is removed to expand the creek bed which also changes the creek's flow somewhat.

Two days later, mining operations go back to what is normal for the miners who are still employed, Daddy being among them. Our family was spared the suffering and loss that many others endured. The muddy and dirty waters made it to our yard but did not invade our home.

The flood was a temporary crisis; the long-lasting crisis was the loss of jobs and homes for people; it was cruel to add to the suffering of people who seemed too pitiful to absorb more hurt, but life abused us. It's as if we were being kicked when we were down.

Minden Flood 1956. Even after rains have stopped and water began subsiding, water continued to run down the hillside. Picture shows how near the railroad track was to some homes.
Picture courtesy of Jane Webb Terry.

7

OUR MOVE

After the flood and the slate dump land slide, more miner families move out and non-miner families begin buying up some of the coal camp houses. These families, fresh to Minden, are unknown to us. I realize the closing of the mines is a catalyst for change, but I feel as if the flood was the straw that broke the camel's back to accepting change.

The mine stays open only one or two days a week worked by a skeleton crew of miners. The coal seam in Minden is dry; it's been extracted of most of its resources. The slate dump's red dog bricks are dwindling. Shabby coal camp houses are left neglected and un-kept waiting for cheap sale.

Our familial heroes, the same men who survived the Great Depression and the War, now have more struggles. Dad and our uncles search for any job they can find. With the numerous mines shutting down simultaneously, there is a swamp full of men looking for work. Dad eventually finds work as a janitor at the Union Hall and the two-room school house, while my brothers continue to deliver newspapers, donating their money to the family funds. I have no idea how we survived with so little money.

Grandpa Apa Vegh and my Uncles Andy and John Vegh raise pigs on Grandpa's land on Pea Ridge Road. When it is time to butcher the pigs, my brothers are called to help. They fill a big barrel full of water, which hangs over an outdoor fire. Once the water is hot, a pig is retrieved from the pen. One of my uncles shoots it between the eyes and hangs the pig in the boiling water to soak. After soaking, the pig is scraped removing any hair prior to butchering. Once butchered, the meat is wrapped and stocked in the freezer.

My brothers gleefully relay the horrible gore, blood and guts story to my sisters and me. Our stomachs feel sick hearing the ghastly stories. The more we show our disgust, the more detail the boys add to their stories. I learned it's best to act as if what they are saying doesn't bother me, but afterwards I refuse to eat pork.

Cheese, powdered eggs, powdered milk, beans and corn meal are distributed to those who lost their jobs. These foods sustain us along with a small garden.

Dad relentlessly searches for another mining job. He says that we need insurance to be sure we can care for Ann and Mama who need special medical care.

Uncle Carl and Aunt Lil Phillips and their daughter Edie buy the small house next to ours on Minden Road. Mama is ecstatic, although she knows we aren't staying in our home. We soon move to another house overlooking the two-room school house and the Union Hall. The new house is bigger than the little five-room house on the road. Mom and Dad bought the house for $3,000, agreeing to monthly payments.

The new house is two-levels and sits on stilts, with seven rooms, including four bedrooms and three porches. The stilts are enclosed providing storage under the house. There are three sets of stairs, one leads up the small knoll in the front yard and two others lead to each side of the front porch. We won't have to worry about future floods. Before we owned it, the house was a duplex.

There are two fireplaces in the home, but Dad has both fireplaces closed off and covered with sheet rock. He says the fireplaces are old and dangerous, and many houses catch on fire due to using old fireplaces. We have seen several house fires in Minden. The houses go up in flames quickly giving off sparks that fly to neighboring homes.

Dad installs an electric furnace in the double doorway between our dining and living rooms. There are no vents, so the heat is not evenly distributed, but it keeps the lower level of the house warm. Another electric heater is installed at the base of the stairs. The house feels much warmer and less drafty than our other home.

We carried our household furniture and belongings by hand, taking a shortcut when possible across the rickety man-made bridge across Arbuckle Creek. Everyone joins in and carries what they can. It is difficult to carry much while walking up the steep hill and then the steps to the house.

The house was vacant for a while before we moved in, so the field mice and rats took residency. Mom and Dad insist the mice and rats must depart before we move in. Mama says that she can't have rats taking bites of her kids while we sleep. She refuses to move in until the rats are gone. They are in the attic and some between the walls, so it takes a while to rid them.

After moving in, I am petrified to go upstairs where the attic entrance leads from a door in the upstairs back bedroom. I adopted Mama's fears of mice and rats. The boys get the upstairs bedrooms where they say they sleep "with one eye open." Dad laughs and assures us that there are no more rats. We see and hear none, so we finally accept they are gone, although in my dreams large deformed rats crawl out of the closet upstairs.

Our neighbors on this hillside are the Rakes family, Mrs. Henderson, and Leach family, none of whom have young children. Mr. Leach is the Vice President of the local United Mine Workers at the time. Daddy worked with all our neighbors at the mine and knows them well.

There are also three Dixon families living nearby, all who have children, which excites us greatly. Uncle John and Aunt Mickey Vegh and our cousins Jon Lee and Dolores live several houses down from us in one direction, and the Wooten family with children our age, Buddy, Tommy and Sue Ann, live on our hill but in the opposite direction.

Below the Wooten family sits the huge Victorian home which once was the doctor's office and our town showcase home that now sits vacant. Rumor is it will soon be a nursing home. Nearby lives the Allen family in a huge house with an enviable level yard that was once the superintendent's home. They have three girls Sherry, Vicki and Sally. We often think how great it would be to have their home since it is so large and near the company store. There are other youngsters that live nearby allowing an endless play group.

My first childhood friend, Alicia Grabosky, moves to the lower end of Minden. Her dad, John Grabosky, manages the water company office in Minden. There are no water meters in town, so everyone pays the same price for water regardless of their usage.

Our group of friends seem to increase on this hill. We spend most of our free time outside. A group of boys make a dam at the bottom of a hill where the spring water flows between the Wooten and Ripoll homes. It is a makeshift pool or watering hole. Some of the boys go skinny dipping to keep their clothes dry. I am promptly sent home. Men in town discover the dam and tell the boys they are worse than beavers as they break it up, leaving the boys to find a new adventure.

Mama continues to read the newspaper daily. She announces that women will now be able to serve on jury duty. Mama works at the voting poles each year and is adamant that it is important to vote. She feels the same way for jury duty, never understanding why women are not allowed to perform this duty the same as men. Mom explains that she's read there are no separate bathrooms for women at the courthouse. For those of us who use outhouses, that seems a feeble excuse. Mama excitedly waits for her chance to participate on a jury, but she is not called.

On a beautiful sunny Sunday afternoon later in the summer, a group of older kids hike down the railroad track. Ann agrees to watch me, so I can join them. Brothers Charles, Robert, and Johnny are there with several neighbor friends. Our group is large. At some point it is decided that we will go to the Rock Lick waterfall. While walking on the railroad track, several of us jump on the rails seeing how far we can run the rails before falling off. Bets are made on who will stay on the longest.

We arrive at the suspended railroad trestle spanning a wide portion of Arbuckle Creek. It's a small trestle but is much too high to jump off. I am frozen with fear, having never seen the trestle up close before. There are no handrails, and the footing is only railroad ties that allow water, rocks, and green scrubs to peek through. Most of our group crossed to the other side without a problem, but I am still inching slowly. Half way across I can go no further. I can't turn back either. I am petrified to move high above the flowing water. I sit motionless clinging to the railroad ties with white knuckles. My brothers shout for me to continue, even offering to help. But I don't want anyone to touch me, convinced I will fall. When I'm on solid ground I am fearless but hovering high above the flowing water I can't drum up the courage to continue.

In desperation, someone yells out that I better move before a train comes barreling down the tracks towards us. Tears run down my cheeks. Ann quickly absolves the threat of being run over by a train since she says trains don't run on Sunday. I wonder if she's right, I can't remember. Finally, I reach a compromise with myself, agreeing to crawl across on my hands and knees, tears dripping on each railroad tie. Once across and still a bit shaken, I stand up ready to move forward. Everyone acts as if nothing happened, sparing further damage to my young ego.

The waterfall is beautiful but not as beautiful as it should be given the distress it took to get there. On our return trip we take the road, not the tracks, to avoid the trestle.

This summer Uncle Johnny, Mama's brother, gives the brothers a huge tent. We call it our circus tent. The boys are excited to have a real tent for camping. The boys pitch the tent in the back part of our yard that borders the woods. Since the yard has a constant upward slant, Dad agrees they can level out the land there. He justifies it by saying the level land can become the horseshoe pit when the tent comes down. The boys spend an entire day shoveling and hauling off dirt until they have a large level section. Then they search for items to fill the tent.

Naturally, I want to join them in the tent. Neither Sue nor Ann have the desire to camp or even hang out in the tent with all those boys. Robert tells me I can join them if I learn a circus act.

"What kind of circus act?" I ask.

"Whatever you want" Robert answers.

I spend hours that day developing a circus act. I try juggling to no avail. In the end, I dress up my cat, Dusty, and suspend a narrow board for us to cross together. Dusty is a gracious cat and cooperates; however, what convinces the boys that I can join is Mama telling them to let me hang out until bedtime. The boys don't argue, and I'm happy with the arrangement. I'm careful to stay quiet causing no problems.

Daddy lets the brothers build a bonfire in a large metal trash can. It is pitch black, country black as we say, with only a few stars that night. It is the end of summer, so the mountain evening is cool. Mama makes hot chocolate and we have marshmallows to roast over the fire. The boys run to the edge of the woods retrieving long sticks to pierce the marshmallows. The fire must be extinguished before Daddy goes to bed.

The boys tell ghosts stories all evening and even seem to be jumpy and jittery now. They keep the sticks they used for marshmallows as protection. Mama left one of the side porch lights on but it's too far to reflect light near the tent. The ground is hard and cool and only a couple of the boys have sleeping bags. The others use blankets. The tent appears to grow larger as the night grows darker.

Mama hollers for me to come inside which I do gladly, while yelling out, "Watch out for snakes or ghosts or maybe a bear," leaving my brothers something to ponder while I'm safe inside the house.

Later that night, Ann recruits me to help her scare the boys. We tell Mama we are going to the toilet. Quiet as field mice, I follow Ann up the hill to the back of the tent. We go to the edge of the woods behind the tent and step on twigs and sticks to make the crackling noise of them breaking. Suddenly, we hear one of the boys holler out hastily, "Is someone there?"

We lower our bodies to the ground and cover our faces to hide from a boy who exited the tent. Not seeing anything, he re-enters, our cue to move quickly and quietly to scratch the back of the tent.

We hear a boy exclaim, "Someone IS out there!"

Another boy surmises, "It may be an animal!"

While the boys are in deep debate on who must go outside to investigate, Ann and I tiptoe down the hillside unseen, slipping back into the house through the side porch.

The next morning the boys wake up early, or by the looks of them they probably stayed up all night. Mom fixes pancakes as they recount to Dad about the animal outside the tent last night. Ann and I restrain the look of victory. The tent remained up on the hillside in the far back portion of our yard for the remainder of summer and early fall.

8

BLACKBERRY PICKIN' AND SNAKES

In 1956, blackberry pickin' is at the top of our list of things to do. It's not just the berry picking, but the camaraderie and adventure of finding a patch before others do when the berries are ripe and at their sweetest. As a bonus, we enjoy delicious blackberry cobblers made with our pickins'.

In the heart of Minden, sitting behind what was once the superintendent's home, is a forgotten little cemetery. Men still gather at the company store, chewing tobacco and smoking cigarettes as they talk. The ones who know us call out to say hi. We wave and holler back to them on our way to the blackberry patch beyond the cemetery. These are the sweetest, largest blackberries ready for picking, so this gold mine must remain a secret.

The cemetery contains the graves of the pioneers of our town, Philip Thurmond who died in 1871 and his wife Mary Thompkins Hill Thurmond who died in 1862, and five of their grandchildren. The Thurmond family settled here over 100 years ago, coming via covered wagon. They had thirteen children and among those were sons William and Philip Thurmond who served in the Civil War as commanders for the Thurmond's Partisan Rangers, a guerrilla troop in the Confederate Army. In those days, this land was part of Virginia. Captain Philip Thurmond was killed in action. Captain William Thurmond returned from the Civil War, settling in Minden on family land. Later he founded the town of Thurmond in the heart of the New River Gorge.

Thurmond is now a ghost town and would eventually be used as a filming location for the movie "Matawan."

When the Arbuckle Creek floods this cemetery is frequently under water, so it is unable to be used for further burials. We are told it is one of the oldest burial grounds in our county and maybe the oldest. Gravesites are lost among the weeds and tall grass, seemingly forgotten. No one comes to this little cemetery anymore.

We imagine when the cemetery was developed this piece of land held endless beauty, especially in the spring with the bursting blooms and scents, and in the fall with the glory of color of reds and oranges and yellows. Then came the coal camp with its little houses and the train track running nearby with the big beasty train coal cars clanging.

My brothers and their friends are excited to get to the blackberry patch. Charles, Robert and John's friends always include Nune Dixon and often Rupert Chuyka and Tommy Wooten. These boys are inseparable. Where you see one, you see the others.

The boys lead the way as Ann and I trail behind laughing and talking. Even though we're anxious to get to the berry patch, we always stop at the gravesites. One of the boys hollers out, "Don't step on any graves!" We hobble along in an attempt not to do so, unsure what may happen if we do.

"What happens if we step on a grave?" I ask while hopping over one nearly losing my balance.

Robert quickly responds, "Mom says it will make the dead person roll over in their grave."

I envision this happening as one of the other boys says, "I heard it stirs up ghosts."

Ann and I see no reason to take a chance as we slowly hop along. Apparently, the boys don't want to take a chance either, all of them carefully stepping around the graves.

Another boy yells in a lazy drawl, "There ain't such things as ghosts."

I wonder why he is jumping over graves then if he doesn't believe in ghosts, but I say nothing. The old grave sites intrigue our curiosity.

It gives us the thrill of exploring, letting our imagination run wild. The haunting adds to the allure of the land. Most of us are sensible and rational, as we have been taught, so exploring our imaginations is entertaining and an escape into a less practical world.

I ask if we can stop to pick wild flowers to put on the graves. The boys agree. One of them calls out, "If there are ghosts, it's good to have them on our side." The rest of us laugh and agree.

A couple of the boys find a blade of grass and place it between their thumbs and whistle a tune as they sit on a nearby rotted tree stump. I have tried endlessly to whistle with a blade of grass but have not been successful. I finally conquered whistling with my hands cupped. Another boy whistles with two fingers in his mouth, making a loud shrill sound. The remainder of us pick wild flowers and lay one on each grave.

We face another obstacle in this overgrown grassy and wet area as we trample through the lush foliage and that is the poison ivy and poison oak with its nasty oil that clings to our bodies regardless of our cautiousness. The itchy rash appears later reminding us of our adventurous exploring. We fear the poison weeds more than the snakes. Now that the flowers are picked and placed on the graves and a few seconds of unspoken silence, we rush off to the blackberry bushes.

Few of us coal camp kids have hiking boots. The shoes we have are severely worn. We are a large family, so we consider ourselves privileged if our shoes have no holes. None of us wear gloves when picking, and no one shows fear of the snakes who seem to love blackberry bushes as much as we do. We put on our oldest clothes since no doubt blackberry stains will be spotting our shirts. We have been scolded from Mama enough times to learn our lesson.

Everyone says snakes lay around blackberry bushes and from prior pickin's we know this is true. Blackberry bushes are a prime area for snakes to hide and wait for crickets, mice or birds. Minden is known to have both copperheads and rattlesnakes and during our adventures we have seen many of both.

The snakes are not aggressive unless they feel threatened. Dad taught us that copperheads attack fast, giving no notice before striking, unlike rattlesnakes that rattle and make a hissing sound to warn you to stay away.

Although I am not scared of the snakes, I certainly respect them enough to stay away. I even avoid black snakes. I'm convinced that if we leave the snakes alone, they will leave us alone. In any case, the blackberries are worth the risk of coming face to face with a snake and the sharp briers that menacingly stick out on the bushes.

We become adept at spotting snakes. We poke sticks into the bushes before picking the berries to scare the snakes away or to bring them out where we can see them. Sometimes it just drives them further into the bushes. It's best to know what you are up against.

We pledge that if a snake slides out of a bush, we will go to another blackberry bush. We don't want to fight the snakes. However, today a snake comes slowly crawling out after our stick poking. The snake doesn't slither away but lies as if it guards the big juicy berries. No one moves. The boys are longingly eyeing the loaded berry bushes.

"Are we going to another spot?" I ask.

"Oh Lordy! Look at all those berries!" one of the boys exclaim, ignoring my question.

One of my brothers suggests, "Maybe the snake will wiggle away," prompting the boys to make noises and continue the stick poking.

Ann yells, "You better not let that snake bite you, Mommy will be mad."

They shush us dismissively, which I can't understand, since they are making so much noise, so why can't we talk? The snake finally slithers away in the opposite direction. The boys are victorious, and rest assured that since it left there must not be a snake den nearby. I'm not so sure.

The thorny blackberry shrubs are mixed with high grass and weeds, further thickening them. The heavy thickets and briers have sharp little teeth, standing ready to grab anything they can dig their thorns into.

It's impossible to avoid the briers and thorns. Our arms and legs are scratched and bleeding. When branches coated with briers snap into our uncovered body parts, we all try to act as if it doesn't hurt, but moaning faces scrunched in pain say otherwise. Sometimes we verbally scold the branches, impatiently waiting for apologies that will never come. I am cautious of the prickly branches behind my brothers that fly back towards my face.

We take turns standing watch for the snake, and hope none of his family is hidden near our feet. We've learned that while pickin', movements must be smooth with no jerks. Your hand never reaches low to the ground without being able to see what is behind the branch. You just leave those berries for the next adventurers, or the snakes.

We talk softly, as if loud voices might disturb the snakes or one of the nearby Thurmonds underground. I'm not sure which scares us the most, the snakes or ghosts. Neither can scare us away from the blackberry bounty. As we leave with stained clothes and hands, bloodied legs and arms with itchy chigger bites and ticks clinging to us, we all agree the blackberry cobbler Mama will make with our loot is well worth it.

Atop the mountain behind the Minden burial ground sits another cemetery, Captain Thurmond's Cemetery, sitting on Pea Ridge Road in Oak Hill. This is the land that was originally Captain William Thurmond's home site. While he was away fighting in the Civil War for the Confederates, his home was burned by the Union Army. When he returned, he moved his home to land that is currently Minden. Thurmond's burial site looks down on the other members of the Thurmond family.

Throughout the remainder of the 1950s and early 1960s, our church youth group spent numerous days tending to both cemeteries, the one in Minden and the one on Pea Ridge Road. To us, the ones buried here are ancient.

We don't know it at the time, the old Thurmond cemetery on Pea Ridge Road becomes part of the sixty-acre Gethsemane Memorial Gardens located in Oak Hill. Over time, a couple of our youth group members will be laid to rest on this peaceful mountaintop. I continue to call it the old Thurmond cemetery.

Our new home has two outhouses on opposite sides of the back yard. The boys are excited that we have an outhouse for the boys and a separate one for the girls. Sue, Ann and I just can't get excited about any outhouse. We want an indoor bathroom, but Daddy says that will have to wait until he gets another mining job.

Daddy trims high grass and scrub bushes regularly taking pride in his yard. This yard is much larger than the one at our old home. This hillside is not rocky like our previous one. The soil is richer, and the grass is greener. Yards on this hillside are sloped, hilly and tidy with green grass.

This year there is a family of copperheads that come out to bask in the sun. Daddy has already killed a couple rattlesnakes in the back yard since he cleared the land. Now a copperhead has been spotted outside the girl's outhouse on several occasions. It crawls and lays outside the door. The snake is fast and seems to sense if one of us or Daddy approaches, so he continues to escape.

One evening I am stuck in the outhouse, screaming and yelling for help. The snake lays outside the door as I stand on top the toilet seat. This must be the largest snake I have ever seen as it seems to grow as I watch it. My heart jumps every time the snake makes a slight movement. Where are the boys? They are always outside playing but no one answers. I hear them playing Tin Can Alley.

My throat is scratchy from yelling for help and a flicker of panic churns through my stomach as I hold back tears. I hate the outhouse more than I do snakes. My forehead is damp from cold sweat. Briefly, I ponder on what to do.

I learn something that evening stuck in the outhouse. I come to the disturbing realization that at times there may not be someone to give me a helping hand or come to my rescue. There has always been, but not today. I must have the courage to pull myself out of situations. This seems to be one of those times.

Being a fast runner, perhaps I can jump over the snake, but I can't get a running start standing in the outhouse. I feel certain the snake will not come after me, but if I make a fast movement, I know it may strike out in self-defense. I try to convince myself that I can wait it out in the toilet, but my patience does not last long.

I have not been afraid of snakes before so why now? The snake has become a predator in my mind, waiting for me. He is on alert due to my screaming, so I decide to be quiet. I study the pros and cons of my dilemma dodging waves of fear. The cold sweat is now running into my eyes, burning. I may have to use the boys' outhouse in the future and pray no snakes find me there.

If the snake decides to crawl into the outhouse, I have no place to run. The fear of being trapped is stronger than my fear of escape. I wait until the snake has moved just a little to the side of the outhouse with his head no longer facing me, but his tail is now in my direction. I swallow my fear, take a deep breath, whisper a quick prayer and jump into a full sprint. Perhaps the next time I must pee, I will take a large stick.

Mommy comes running out to see what all the yelling is about, the brothers not far behind her. I look back to see the snake slithering off in the opposite direction. I yell out in a quivering and weak voice, "Where were y'all when I needed you?" Feeling my legs somewhat wobbly, I quickly scan the area then sit down in the grass as I try to hold back tears already rolling to my cheeks. The snake shows himself again occasionally, but we never catch him.

Under the wooden steps that lead up the little knoll to our front yard, a snake sits patiently, preventing anyone from walking up our steps. Daddy isn't home so Squeaky decides he will handle the situation. His solution is to burn and smoke the snake out from under the steps. There are dried leaves under the steps. Squeaky catches the steps on fire in his attempt to smoke out the snake. The snake crawls away while the boys flail around in a state of panic.

When Daddy comes home, Squeaky excitedly reports his accomplishment on how he forced the snake away from the steps, "The snake kept everyone from walking up the steps, so I burned it out!" Daddy listens intently, then looks down to the charcoaled wooden steps partially disintegrated.

He responds, "We don't have to worry about the snake hiding under those steps anymore."

There are girl cousins, Jon Lee and Dolores, and neighbor, Joy Dixon, on our hill so I finally have girl playmates my age. Jon Lee and Dolores love to swing on the real swing set, not a tire tied to a tree, in their yard. We spend many summer afternoons on the swings, at times we swing so high that the post comes off the ground causing Aunt Mickey to run outside.

However, better than the swing set are the vines that grow on trees in the woods. We search for these vines to swing. Even Ann joins in, but she is older and has her own friends who are more interested in boys, polishing their nails and fixing their hair, than swinging on vines with a bunch of little girls.

Currently, Ann has her eye on Tommy Dixon, a handsome dark wavy-haired boy who lives around the hill. He is cute with an easy, warm and inviting smile.

One afternoon, Ann had me iron her hair on the ironing board. I keep asking her, "You sure you want me to do this? I don't even know how to iron clothes!"

Ann lays her long curly hair on the ironing board and has me put a towel over her hair, so the iron doesn't burn it. Mama comes in the room and hollers at both of us. It startled me so badly I jumped and almost hit Ann in the head with the iron. Ann turned and looked at me with a grimace, but I don't dare chuckle. One side of her hair now hangs longer and straighter while the other side curls over her shoulder. Ann pleads with Mama to let me iron the other side, but Mom refuses claiming her hair might fall off. One of the boys holler that Tommy Dixon is on the front porch waiting for Ann. She throws a towel over her head and runs to the bedroom pretending she is not home.

I call out, "I think he heard you say you weren't at home, Ann."

As mama says, "Well, Sissy, if he didn't hear her, he surely heard you."

The boys say us girls are such strange creatures. Ann wants her hair straight, but I want mine curly. Mama gives me a hair permanent every summer before school starts to get my hair curlier.

One afternoon my girl buddies, Jon Lee, Dolores and I decide to roam into the nearby woods behind their house. We have walked through the woods to Grandma and Grandpa Vegh's house many times. Today we three girls feel confident and adventurous and more mature than our age as we explore the woods. Aunt Mickey thinks we are playing on the swing set. Eventually our expedition at the edge of the woods turns off the familiar pathway, leading us deeper into the woods than normal. We see no familiar landmarks, just thick foliage and underbrush. There is no sign of houses in any direction, and we are totally void of what direction we should walk. Our roaming had spiraled needlessly out of control. Not only are we lost, but we know we will be in trouble, too.

We start hollering hoping someone will hear us as we hold on tight to each other. We were foolish to think we knew our way through the woods. We yell again, louder this time with combined voices. Suddenly, a dog barks. It's their dog. He heard us. Continuing to yell, we walk towards the barking. We run through the dried leaves left from last year and avoid broken branches. The trees are in full bloom and thicker, making it difficult to see very far. Finally, we catch a glimpse of houses far below. We are safe. The dog is our hero. We run to embrace him with hugs, his tongue generously passes out licks.

We watch the boys some nights sit quietly together, scheming a new adventure or prank. Mom tells Daddy she knows the boys are up to something.

Dad replies, "Liz, they are just sitting there," but I think Daddy knows something is not right.

Mom tells Daddy that he needs to get down there and see what they are up to. As Daddy approaches, the boys scatter in a panic. One of the neighbors has an adult daughter visiting and at dusk she stands in her bedroom to change clothes without pulling down the window shade.

Daddy is persistent in searching for another coal mining job and it finally pays off. He gets a mining job at a small non-union mine in Raleigh County. Daddy does not like that it is a non-union mine offering no health insurance, and it doesn't pay as much as he is used to, but it pays more than being a janitor. We are one of the fortunate families with Daddy finding another mining job quickly. Since we don't have a vehicle, Daddy walks over the hill to Salem Road in Oak Hill to catch a ride with another miner he knows.

Daddy works the night shift at the new mine. His pace has slowed. He smiles and says that he enjoys his walks outside to work, but we overhear Daddy tell Mama that he doesn't know how long the job will last. Rumor is that the coal is getting scarce at the coal seam.

Minden Coal Miners.

9

DEATH OF A COAL CAMP ERA

It's painful to watch something die, something that you love and cherish. It's agonizing to lose what has been part of you for as many years as you are. The changes that began in 1955, compounded by the flood in 1956, slowly caused our town as we knew it to fade away piece by piece each time another coal camp family moved away. The town never reaches the desertion level of being a ghost town, but the spirit of the coal camp era faded away as the town took on its new form.

Coal was out for our town, but the space race was booming. NASA is newly formed flourishing new hopes and new challenges. We are excited that someday we may travel to the moon. Since most of us have seldom been outside of Minden, the moon seems as attainable as any other place we see on television.

We don't fear change anymore. It's happened. We accept the loss of our way of life and begin to embrace change with a sense of hope. As kids, our adventures continue regardless.

Dewey Pittman, a young pastor and school teacher, who grew up in Rock Lick, has strong ties to the town and often assists with the youth group. He loves Minden and Rock Lick. On one afternoon, Dewey takes a group of youth to the slate dump or what is left of it since the flood, to make one of his films.

As much as I dislike the slate dump, I go along with Ann and my brothers, and Nune and Rupert, to watch the filming. The slate dump forever gives me chilly goose bumps. The slate dump is barren, it hasn't been used recently, but heat still radiates from it. I see a group of young people wearing white robes carrying a cross, singing loudly as Dewey films. The white robes flow as the gentle breeze blows, giving a ghostly effect.

Looking around, I notice other young people watching quietly as the white robed youth march to the beat of the music. I am told Dewey wants the audience to feel a spiritual connection with the contrast between the white robes and black slate. To me it is eerie, and I'm anxious to leave.

My brothers often go to Thurmond with our Uncle Johnny to fish on the banks of the New River. Uncle Johnny lost his mining job as well and now works at a gas station in Oak Hill until he finds another job. He and my brothers fish more often than they used to. The boys get up early to dig for worms before the long walk along the railroad track to Thurmond. Thankfully it is mostly a downhill slope, and they hitch a ride back to avoid that long uphill walk. I've been allowed to go to the river a couple times, but only when a group of church kids go to picnic on the sandy bank. Many of us don't swim well, but it doesn't stop us from jumping on inner tubes to float near the riverbanks.

Summer days turned to Fall, bringing out the exotic colors of the mountainsides. We wake to school and cool mornings. Daylight is shorter. Fall then turns into cold snowy winters with temperatures plummeting. Cold winds blow and snow falls, icicles hang from porches. With snow on the ground, we search for sleds, boxes, or pieces of tin to make a sleighing device. No hill escapes our sleighing. We leave the hillsides too slick to climb.

One afternoon, I join my siblings and our group of friends sliding down the hill. Each of us have a piece of tin or a cardboard box. I fly down the hill on a piece of tin that seemingly sprouts wings, I'm going so fast. Laughing in pure pleasure, I close my eyes to avoid the snow flying back into my face. I hear my friends hollering for me to jump off. Opening my eyes for a split second, I see the creek quickly approaching. I instantly roll off the tin landing in a pile of snow at the creek bed, the tin plunging into the freezing creek water.

Nighttime sledding is our favorite as the moonlight shimmers over the snow. Sometimes on snowy weekends when there is a big moon, Daddy builds a bonfire for us as we sled down the hill while Mama makes homemade cookies and hot chocolate. Everyone is soaked through, freezing as the icy wind pierces our clothes. Daddy must physically restrain us from trudging up the hill to sled down again.

Winter brings our favorite time of the year - the Christmas holidays. The company store stocks the second floor with toys for all ages; it's open for its last Christmas Toyland. Everyone enthusiastically checks out the new merchandise. We swarm the store like honeybees. We don't allow ourselves the luxury of dreaming for many of these items, as we know they will not be under our tree.

The United Mine Workers Union has a Christmas celebration for the members' children with Santa, who passes out bags of goodies at Union Hall. These goodies are little brown pokes filled with fruit, candy and nuts, which we graciously accept with the upmost excitement. This year is our last Christmas at the Union Hall with Santa.

Our church hosts Christmas plays, and the youth group sings Christmas carols to older members who live nearby. The church also passes out goodie bags to all children attending Christmas Sunday service. Mama usually helps prepare the goodie bags. Like the Union, the goodies are little brown pokes filled with fruit and candy.

The festivities continue from Thanksgiving through New Year's Day. At home, Mama bakes homemade breads, pies, cakes and fudge. Fresh fruits and nuts are plentiful in our home during the holiday season.

It's a tradition in our family to venture into the woods to find a special Christmas tree. We scout trees during our summer hikes, making a point to remember where to go back during winter. We head out early, following the steep trails with rising elevation, looking for our perfect Christmas tree. It takes hours to find the tree, cut it down and drag it back home.

When we get home, our tree is always too tall for the house, and one side is usually bare, but it can be easily trimmed. With careful placement the bare spot is hidden towards the back. We only have a few strings of lights, but to us the tree glows bright. The best part, an angel sits on top the tree. The house smells of fresh pine and homemade cookies.

We collect extra pine branches and mistletoe to decorate the porches, stringing the lighted pine branches around the door frame, and hanging mistletoe over the front entry.

It will be a happy Christmas.

Sue has a date who comes to our home to pick her up bringing a gift wrapped in bright silver paper. Ann and I stand in the dining room pretending to work on a puzzle while listening to their conversation.

I quietly say to Ann, "Look at that, he wrapped her present in aluminum foil. Think he doesn't have enough money to buy wrapping paper?"

"Oh, my gracious, Sissy!" Ann replies. "That's not aluminum foil. It's wrapping paper."

"Wrapping paper! Really?"

After the holiday season, the long winter hangs around longer than we like.

Then comes the day our company store closes its doors for the last time. While sitting on our front porch, Dad reaches into his pocket, digging for something. Mom handles the finances, but Daddy has a few coins in his pocket. He hands me a coin, and hands Mom the others. It's a scrip coin issued by the coal company, worn and almost unreadable. I tell Daddy that we can't spend coal company coins now that the company store closed for good. Daddy advises me to save the coin because "Someday it may be valuable. They won't be making these coins anymore." Daddy tells Mama to put her script coins in their cedar chest where they save all things of value. I hide my well-worn scrip coin in my jewelry box I received for Christmas.

The train whistles that once brought life and enchantment into our little community, rarely sound anymore. It saddens us to no longer hear the train whistle.

The beautiful huge Victorian home, once a doctor's office, is now a faded nursing home. After the doctor's office closed, the house sat vacant before fire ravaged it. The house was eventually repaired and converted into a nursing home. My brothers and their friends try to convince me that ghosts haunt the old Victorian house, even more so now that people die there.

Our church youth group visits the nursing home to sing to the residents. I know we don't sound very good, possibly barely adequate. It probably helps that many of those listening can't hear us anyway. Most of us have never visited a nursing home prior to our choral trip. All the older folks we know are still spry. We are shocked to see the elderly sitting in wheelchairs with self-absorbed stares, seemingly unaware of their surroundings. Residents with dementia call out to us thinking we are their family. A few joyful residents enjoy our singing and ask us to return.

The brothers are sure that upstairs is where the ghosts roam freely. My eyes dart back and forth towards the stairs, but I'm not the only one. I notice other youngsters keep an eye on those stairs ready to flee if necessary. I'm relieved when our visit is over. Afterwards I dream of ghosts floating down the Victorian stairs chasing us out the front door. Mama and Daddy tell the boys to quit talking nonsense about ghosts to the younger kids, but the damage has already been done.

For years, as I passed the old Victorian beauty I kept an eye on the windows just to make sure no ghosts appear. My mind tries to play tricks on me visualizing a curtain moving in one of the windows revealing a partial face. Is this a real person? Or is my imagination overactive? In my mind the curtain drops still, never giving me a straight answer.

Some of the coal camp houses are left abandoned when they do not sell. Some houses caught on fire and are left in ruins. The most dilapidated were torn down. The houses that did sell are inhabited by new people, not miners, but others looking to lay down roots in a new place. Many houses breathe new life with a colorful coat of paint in vibrant hues.

Daddy continues working at the small non-union mine in Raleigh County, regularly checking with the union and old friends for news of union mines that may be hiring. He continues to walk over the hilltop to Salem Road each morning and back each evening, never complaining, but showing signs of obvious weariness.

By 1957, Squeaky graduated high school, and is the last year he lived at home. Along with other young men from Minden and Oak Hill, he joined the Army to travel the world. Squeaky is excitedly anticipating a lively new world and is thrilled to see where it will take him. Squeaky is the first kid in our family to escape the hard life of a coal camper.

By 1958, our sister Sue is a senior in high school and starts her first job as a reporter at the <u>Fayette Tribune</u> in Oak Hill. We are extremely proud of her; she has always wanted to be a reporter, and through hard work she achieved her dream. That same year, Sue co-writes a book with Robert Holliday, editor of the Oak Hill <u>Fayette Tribune</u>. The book is published by <u>The Montgomery Herald</u> newspaper and entitled, *"About Montgomery West Virginia."* She pours herself into her work, spending long hours on the job and comes home most nights with new tidbits of information to pass on to us.

Aunt Edie, Mommy's sister, continues to drive Mom and Ann to Charleston to see Ann's cardiologist. I ride along with them to avoid being under the care of my brothers. I love Charleston's large buildings, traffic going in all directions, people walking the streets, the gold capitol dome, the shops and restaurants, and the Kanawha River running through the city. I am in complete awe. Charleston is another world from our coal town. A world that I would like to know. Driving back home, Mom gladly announces that the doctor said Ann is doing great. Ann proudly smiles.

Late, when Mommy thinks no one is listening, I overhear her tell Daddy that there will come a time when Ann will need surgery. Thankfully not today, but some day.

With the company store permanently shuttered, Mr. Bates continues to open his porch store for a bit. While we are walking to the Bates' store, we spot the last of train's beasty cars sitting idle on the track. We walk over to jump on them.

Never again will there be coal trains to hop on, hitching a free ride down the track to the company store. Jumping the train is not an easy feat. It takes perfect timing, the precise moment to jump when the train slowed to labored chug preparing to pick up or drop off the coal cars. We were ridiculously reckless and impulsive at times. Heaven forbid that an adult sees us jump on or off the train. Our Mama would surely rake us over the coals.

Vicki Allen, a childhood friend, recounted a story that her mama saw our friend Alicia Grabosky hanging off the side of the train. Vicki's mom called Alicia's mom to tell her.

On our last coal car adventure, we open the sliding door of one of the beasts, tasting the coal, and are buzz-bombed by bats. We screamed in terror. We are all going to miss the train, Minden just won't be the same without it.

On our way home, the boys go to Nune's house. I decide to look for my cat Dusty to keep me company. I found a little kitten one day when we first moved to our new house on the hill, and immediately fell in love with it. Mama occasionally allows Dusty in our house, which no other pet has had the privilege to enter. Dusty quite likes the outdoors, so it's all the same to him.

Dusty is my companion when the boys are occupied with their friends, and my sisters are off doing whatever older sisters do. As a kitten, Dusty allowed me to dress him in doll clothes and push him around in a doll carriage pretending to drink from a baby bottle. When he had enough meddling, he jumped out of the carriage and ran up the old maple tree in our front yard. I soon start climbing the tree to go after him.

As an adult cat, he continues to humor me and when he tires of my antics, he climbs higher in the tree to escape. I climb higher, too. Like Dusty, I can sit in the tree peacefully for hours enjoying my high perch above my sibling's activities below. Eventually Mom yells for me to climb down the tree. She's scared I will break a bone. I figure Dusty will come down when he is ready.

One day I call for Dusty, but he does not come running. Mom and Dad share my surprise, joining me in calling for him. Mom thinks he is hiding high in the tree to avoid playing with me, but I searched the tree from top to bottom not finding Dusty lounging in the branches.

The search moves to the back yard. I find him lying in the shade near a lilac bush, unable to move and foaming at the mouth. I squat on the grass beside him, scared that if I touch him I will hurt him. Fear crawls up my body. I scream for help and Daddy comes running.

I beg Daddy to help save Dusty. Daddy kneels over him looking at my companion, then turns to me as he says, "I can't, Sissy. He can't be helped now."

Tears stream out of my eyes. Daddy puts his arm around my shoulders and says, "Go sit on the front porch with your Mommy, and I will stay with Dusty."

"He's dying, isn't he?"

Daddy shakes his head up and down. "I can stay with him too? He's probably scared. What's wrong with him?" I sob.

Daddy replies, "It looks like he ate poison."

"Poison? Where would he get poison?"

Daddy answers, "I don't know."

We sit on the grass with Dusty. Daddy mowed the grass earlier that afternoon and the smell of freshly cut grass lingers in the air. I hear the birds chirping their evening songs. My hands shake as I softly pet him, and my heart feels an aching pain like someone stuck a dull spike in it. It's difficult to catch my breath. This unexpected life experience nearly knocks the breath out of me as my anxiety heightens. Daddy sits calmly beside me switching his eyes from Dusty to me.

I ask Daddy, "Cats go to heaven too, don't they?"

Daddy looks at me and answers, "Yes, I reckon so, Sissy."

The wait is short. Daddy and I bury Dusty at the far end of the back yard. Afterwards, I go to the old Oak tree in our front yard and climb to the top. It was difficult for me to understand the intensity of what I was feeling. There was a deep sadness I had not experienced. I just wanted things the way they were. I wanted my cat back.

Charles, Robert and Johnny come walking home with their friend Nune, carrying parts of old bicycles. Under Johnny's arm are comic books which he has scrunched tightly to not drop them. You seldom see Johnny without his comic books these days. He most likely just traded some with one of the other boys. No wonder he won the school spelling contest. They may only be comic books, but he still reads a lot.

Robert sadly told us that Nune's family will be moving soon. Nune doesn't want to move, but he must. He loves this town and his friends. The boys have been inseparable most their lives. All of us are going to miss him.

The brothers go into the enclosed section under the porch to drop off their bicycle parts which they store beside our lawnmower and other outdoor tools. Daddy doesn't allow the yard to be messy. Everything must be put up when they finish working. Robert, Charles and Johnny have a knack for working on bicycles, especially Robert. The boys rebuilt most of our bicycles from scrap bike parts, so we all have bicycles. I must ride near the house, which means the roads are made of bumpy red dog, making bike riding difficult. The bike wrecks leave me with scarred knees and elbows.

From my high perch in the old oak tree, I watch the boys work, talk and laugh, making jokes. They swat at a mosquito that is flying around them. One brother swatted a little harder than necessary, causing the conversation tone to rise as a few friendly shoves were passed back and forth, followed by laughter.

At the sound of female laughter, I turn my head to see Ann and one of her friends walking up the newly built steps to our house. Tommy Dixon is walking down the red dog road towards them, waving and yelling, "Hello! Hello!"

Smiles cross the girls' faces. Our simple, busy activities continue all around me, only I don't have Dusty. Although I have my brothers and sisters, I still feel alone with a sharp ache in my heart.

Still sitting in my tree, a thought pops into my head. I think about Mom and Dad, and how they must worry about Ann being sick. I quickly learn that an aching and sad heart is heavy, difficult to carry. How do they manage, I wonder?

Mom yells for me from the porch, "Sissy, are you going to go find some wildflowers for Dusty?"

I sadly respond, "I don't see any blooming."

She offers, "You can have a rose from my rose bushes."

"Really?" I slowly climb down the tree. Mom goes inside to retrieve the scissors and joins me in the yard. Her roses are her guarded treasures.

Later this year we get a surprise. Daddy gladly informs us he finally found a union coal mining job in Raleigh County at Eccles working for the Winding Gulf Coals, Inc. Dad is one of the fortunate coal miners that locates another union mining job without uprooting his family. *Dad will work this mine until he retires.*

He and Mama love their town and their friends. They don't seem to have noticed that it's not the same, or perhaps they just don't show it. Faith and persistence paid off for Daddy. He never gave up trying.

Mom, smiling with pride, quietly asks, "Will we have insurance?"

Daddy replies, "Yes, Liz, we will."

After which I immediately exclaim, "Can we have an indoor bathroom now?"

Daddy's smile erupts like a volcano, and answers, "Yes, we can!"

10

THE SCRAPBOOK

Summer, July 2016. As we continue our road trip to our family reunion in West Virginia, my phone rings pulling me out of my reminiscing. I answer, my brother Charles calls out, "Where are you, Sis?"

"We're crossing the state line" I respond. "Are we the last ones?"

"No. I just wanted to let you know that we took our truck load of donations to the church. Paquita met us there."

Charles and his wife Sandy also brought in a truck load of donations. Paquita, a coal camp kid that grew up with my sister Sue, still attends our childhood church, the Minden Missionary Baptist Church. She married a childhood friend Kenny Sarver, and they live in Oak Hill but still attend the Minden church.

"I'm assured the church will see that the donations are given to those affected by the flood." Charles says.

"Yes, I'm sure they will. When am I to take our truckload?" I ask.

"You can take it Sunday when the family attends church."

As part of the family reunion, we will fill the pews in the little church that Mom and Dad loved so dearly. It was a big part of each of our lives. Our pastor during the early years was Reverend Finley Prewitt. As the mines began closing and people moved away, the church lost members including Pastor Prewitt. In 1959, a young pastor named Reverend James Mundy became pastor of our church. Unknowing to us at the time, Jim Mundy later becomes our brother-in-law, marrying our sister Sue. After Mom and Dad's deaths, we youngsters had a stained-glass window installed at the church in their memory.

Palmer and I finally cross the West Virginia state line. I peer up to our majestic, gorgeous mountains. Unlike city buildings and architectural structures, man can't take credit for the God-given beauty of these mountains. I feel "Mountaineer" pride. We are greeted by hills and hollows as we continue and, if we would get off the beaten track of the interstate and go down the road "a spell" we would pass abandoned mining towns and what use to be coal country.

We travel through Greenbrier County, the county ravaged by the historic 100-year flood recently. The tranquil valley of White Sulphur Springs spreads beneath the Allegheny Mountains and is often hit with floods, but the most recent flood was one for the ages.

A cousin on our maternal side, Sylvia, my Aunt Helen's daughter, sent me an email a few days after the flood. She no longer lives in West Virginia but grew up as a coal camp kid the same as me. In her email she said she was visiting The Greenbrier Resort while in town for her Nuttall High School class reunion when the flood hit. I pick up my phone to read Sylvia's message again:

> *"We drove through Rainelle, and water rose rapidly. We were trapped in Rupert overnight after a car was swept away in front of us."*

The Greenbrier Resort is a historic, luxury resort with 700 rooms. It dates to 1778 and is a registered historic landmark having hosted numerous Presidents and dignitaries. When I was a child I thought this resort held mysteries and beauty I would never get to experience, even though we lived relatively close.

The Greenbrier is best known for its secret underground bunker, which of course, is no longer secret. The bunker was designed by the government as an emergency shelter for Congress. The secret was revealed when its discovery was printed in <u>The Washington Post</u>. Now, I suppose, the government has built a bunker in another secret location.

Built during the Cold War, the bunker was the ultimate bomb shelter. Little did we know that the hills of West Virginia contained such an important national security location.

During World War II, the Greenbrier was home to German and Japanese detainees deemed to be possible enemies. The Army later commandeered the resort as a hospital. The Greenbrier then and still today is gorgeous and a sheer delight to visit.

The week after the historic flood, the Greenbrier Resort was scheduled to host the PGA *Greenbrier Classic* golf tournament. The television stations showed the lush golf course covered with mud, debris and severed trees brought from the floodwaters. Instead of hosting the tournament, the resort was closed to paying guests for a few weeks while they recovered from the devastation brought by the flood. The repair of the golf courses would take much longer. However, the resort was not closed completely, it generously opened its doors to flood victims. Whenever I pass The Greenbrier, I know I'm not far from home.

As we near our destination, I reach for my Mom's scrapbook which I brought along. Usually, I keep it tucked away on my book shelf. It's a treasure trove of information. As I open it, out falls faded newspaper articles and pictures. Mom and Dad were avid readers of the local newspapers. I cautiously pick up the fragile newspaper articles, and carefully insert them back into the album. I fight back a sudden jolt of sadness as I remember my youth.

For a while, long after the closing of the Minden mines, Mom wrote a small column in the local newspaper, the <u>Fayette Tribune</u>, titled *"Minden and Rock Lick"* by Mrs. Buster Crone or otherwise known as the *"Minden Mailbox."* Her home phone number was published as the contact. Mom, shy to newcomers but a social creature by nature, loved her newspaper column, through which she reported the Minden local news, who visited who, births, parties, church activities, or whatever social function a resident wants to advertise.

If Mom was here, I reckon she would still be talking my ears off, telling me what everyone is doing, sharing a little gossip and the latest news of small and inconsequential things.

Throughout the album, she neatly displayed the articles. On some she forgot to write the date of the article. Among the articles, are a couple news clips on our Uncle Jake, Dad's youngest brother. Uncle Jake ended his coal miner career several years before the Minden mine closed. I was too young to remember. News traveled fast that one of the Crone boys was injured. Dad rushed to the accident site where he sadly discovered that his brother Jake did not survive the accident. He died shortly before his 40th birthday. When Jake pulled the cord on the machine he was operating, the cord snapped and wrapped around his neck, breaking it.

There are several newspaper articles on the old Minden Cemetery. The Wonderland Garden Club, later known as The Wonderland Civic Club of Minden, restored the old cemetery. Mama served on this committee along with many long-time resident women, such as Yvonne Arthur, Henrietta Brellahan, Lorrainne Bowyer, Mrs. Eugene Dixon, Pauline Evans, Lucille Miller, Lillian Phillips, Virginia Watkins, and Ann Watters. The cemetery is one of the oldest in Fayette County, and the one we visited as kids when blackberry pickin'.

Palmer calls out that we are fast approaching Beckley. We are just about twenty minutes from my hometown. Beckley has expanded over the years with new shopping and restaurants, bringing increased traffic and congestion on roads never designed to service so many people.

Each time I visit Beckley, there appears to be something new added. One of Beckley's tourist attractions is The *Exhibition Coal Mine*, a museum and a re-created coal camp. When I visit the exhibition, it's as if I step back in time to my childhood.

I focus on the scenery for the remainder of the trip, taking inventory of any changes. As we approach Oak Hill, I notice that it seems to seldom change. I have a special love for this town. I spent my high school and teenage years in Oak Hill.

"We're almost there!" I announce, as if Palmer doesn't already know. Before I can say more, my phone rings with my son J.J. calling wondering where we are.

"We'll be there soon" I say.

11

THE REUNION

July 2016. We pull up to the Holiday Lodge in Oak Hill. Outside are a group of older nephews and nieces with their kids headed to grab food at a local restaurant. My siblings and I are now the older generation. Our children, the younger generation, planned the family reunion this year. We take immense pride in them, and their kids. Our roots run deep and branch out to many areas these days, but our hearts will always be rooted in Oak Hill.

Rebecca, Sharon and Penny call out to us. Rebecca, my niece and Robert's daughter, does a marvelous job organizing the reunion and Squeaky's son, David and his wife Andi, organized this year's family games. Two of our nieces, Penny, our sister Sue's daughter, and Lisa, our brother Robert's daughter, will not be able to join us at the reunion. Both have breast cancer and are in the middle of treatment.

We don't know it at the time of the reunion, but neither Penny nor Lisa will join us at a future reunion. Both lose their battles with cancer in the coming year. Large families bring much love and joy, and much heartache and sadness, too.

We go inside to check-in, and the hotel lobby is bursting alive with family members, some sitting and talking in a huddle, while others congregate around the fireplace area playing cards. Many of the younger generation have only met each other on a few occasions, but all accept each other freely as family and instantly make friends with distant cousins.

The hotel staff does not object to our lobby takeover. In the distance, I hear a familiar ring of laughter. It warmly settles over me. J.J., Christy, Connor and Garrett are in the pool area. They live in my neighborhood in Virginia, just a street away, so I see them often, but I still run excitedly to say "Hi". Christy and J.J. are relaxing pool side while Connor and Garrett are embattled in a hot game of water volleyball with people in the pool. I smile.

It will be good to see everyone at the reunion tomorrow. This year we are gathering at Hawk's Nest State Park.

Back in the lobby, Squeaky, who in his older age transitioned from Squeaky to Gene, gives me a big hug. "Want to join us at cards?"

"I just got here, so I'll pass." Gene is an older version of Squeaky, moving a bit slower now, but his personality hasn't changed much. Gene never shows his age; he looks and acts much younger than his real age. He looks very much like Dad, with the same generous and kind heart.

It's debatable which brother is the hardest worker these days, as they all are workaholics. Generally, Gene holds the hardest working title, both for good work ethics and having the most children in the family but all the brothers have been hard workers. Having owned several successful businesses, Squeaky continues to work. He says he will retire someday.

We greet other nephews and nieces and cousins, passing out hugs and hellos. We haven't seen some since the last reunion two years ago.

Palmer's youngsters, Palmer III and Lilli, cannot make the reunion this year both having started new jobs.

Robert and Johnny rush over to give me a hug. My four brothers and I live in Virginia, only a few hours from one another. We make a priority of getting together every few months to have a "sibling day" with just us and our spouses. Sometimes we plan a weekend getaway, anything to stay in touch.

I would like to say that we outgrew picking on one another, but what fun would that be? When we all get together, the immaturity comes out in all of us.

Looking at Robert is like looking at Mom and her Hungarian family. His dark curly hair is now streaked with more gray than black.

He still exudes the same persuasive smile and charm that he did in his youth. His stories and tall tales continue to befuddle us, wondering if they are true or not. He's still the life of the party. Robert became a building engineer and pursued further certifications, eventually retiring as a Regional Director for the company. He gave up his bicycle repair hobby, replacing it with a vicious habit and hobby of collecting unique cars to buy and sell. Like Squeaky, Robert has inexhaustible energy. He holds the runner up title of having the most children.

Johnny, the quietest, youngest brother, stands the tallest, with an enviable thin build and those bold blue eyes. He still never argues with any of us and is always there when we need him. He walks with a limp now from wilder days of riding motorcycles followed years later by a car accident that left him having multiple surgeries. When I look at him I see our Uncles Andy and John. Johnny retired after spending his adult life as a butcher for union grocery stores.

Standing in the lobby surrounded by family, young and old, it feels good to be here. Tomorrow brings the reunion and even more family, games, food and memories.

I hear my brother Charles call out as he brings along with him the hotel night manager, telling her she must meet their baby sister. Charles is no longer that reddish-blond headed, lanky boy with freckles covering his face, often getting into mischief. Now we call him the banker and social director. He earned both titles and would not even consider any mischief today. He served in the Army followed by a lustrous career in finance and banking, from which he eventually retired. His social directorship is a family title, having been stuck with the duties of organizing family functions for years. He tries to hide from that duty, but we don't allow it.

Robert puts his arm around my shoulders and says to me, "We've been waiting on you, Sis. Come on. It's going to be a busy weekend so we're going to go see Sue and Ann before it gets too hectic. We have some friends stopping by the hotel tomorrow, too."

Robert and Johnny beckon the other siblings. Squeaky and his wife Bonnie, Charles and his wife Sandy, Robert and his wife Janice, Johnny and his wife Diana, and Palmer and I jump in vehicles. Robert drives as Squeaky sits shotgun. Charles hollers out that the rest of them will follow in his car.

"Let's go see Sue first," Squeaky says.

We turn off on Pea Ridge Road leading to the old Thurmond cemetery, as Robert proudly announces, "I brought the flowers!"

We know we will not find Sue or Ann when we go to visit, just their memories, as they have moved on. We continue to miss them with an ache in our hearts, but we know one day we will be reunited.

Crone 2016 Family reunion. Picture courtesy of Rebecca Crone.

12

MINDEN, YESTERDAY AND TODAY

This picture is of the upper end of Minden before Scrapper's Corner. On the small hilltop to the right, sits the Saint Casimir Catholic Church which was established as a mission of the Scarbro Saints Peter and Paul Church. The Saint Casimir Catholic Church was torn down.

Originally, the land known as Minden was called Arbuckle and the creek was called Arbuckle Creek, named after two brothers that lived on the land as squatters. The land was owned by Captain Thurmond who sold the mineral rights to a coal operator named Paddy Rend who established the mining town of Rend in 1899.

Later another coal operator named Edward J. Berwind purchased Rend's mineral rights and Thurmond's land, changing the name of the town to Minden. Berwind named the town after his mother's home town, Minden, Germany. Minden celebrates it's official birth year as 1905.

By 1923, the New River and Pocahontas Consolidated Coal Company, the name in which Berwind operated his mining business, had three mines in Minden: No. 2, No. 3 and No. 4 and employed 649 men. Later there was a No. 5 mine opened.

Local Union No. 5949 of the United Mine Workers of America, District No. 29 was chartered in Minden in 1932.

Minden continued to prosper and had one of the most productive coal seams in the New River Coal Field. Its smokeless high quality bituminous coal was in high demand. Over 2000 people resided in the town at its peak.

By 1955, most of the coal had been extracted and the mines began shutting down. Some miners remained working a few years longer to extract the remaining coal and complete the closure of the mines. The closure happened gradually over several years.

Today, some of the original coal camp homes still exist. The Crone coal camp house located near Scrapper's Corner no longer stands. The lot sits empty. The company store, the doctor's office and the two-room school house with the attached Union Hall no longer stand. The original post office is also gone; a new one was constructed in a different location.

Pictures from top left: Doctor's Office which turned into a Nursing Home after the mines closed and later into apartments, Minden Missionary Baptist Church (located at lower end of Minden), Minden Company Store, Minden coal tipple, and coal train.

Members of the Minden Reunion Committee host a small reunion annually for the old-timers who previously lived in Minden and its current residents. The Minden reunion is held every Labor Day weekend. Attendance dwindles as time goes by.

During the 1980s and 1990s, PCB contamination was discovered from Shaffer Equipment Company who operated in Minden. Although the contamination began much earlier, up until the late 1970s, PCB contamination was not a concern. Popular belief was that the remediation of the area was completed; however, there continues to be an investigation into whether all areas were remediated.

> U.S. v. Shaffer Equipment Co., Nos. 92-2024, 93-1007, and 93-1049, United States Court of Appeals, Fourth Circuit. Argued May 4, 1993. Decided December 9, 1993. States in part:

> *"Shaffer Equipment Company, a firm in Minden, West Virginia, was engaged in the business of rebuilding electrical substations for the local coal mining industry, which involved the storing and disposing of transformers and capacitators on its property. Shaffer Equipment also modified transformers for customers, which often involved disposing of residual transformer fluid. Evidence revealed that while some of the fluid was simply poured onto the ground, the predominant practice was to store the fluid in drums and containers at the site, some of which later deteriorated and leaked fluid onto the ground. In response to a complaint, West Virginia authorities and the EPA tested soil samples from the site and discovered that the soil at the site was contaminated with polychlorinated biphenyls ("PCB's"). Because of the risk to persons in the area, the EPA regarded the site as hazardous and in need of remediation."*

According to a recent broadcast on WOAY TV, this matter still greatly concerns the residents.

> "Doctor Says Chemical Stored in Abandoned Mine Causes Cancer in Minden" by Rebecca Fernandez, May 10, 2017 as stated in part below:

"This is a list of over 212 families, out of 250 in Minden, West Virginia who have had at least one member of their family diagnosed with cancer over the last 25 years."

There are several articles published in the local newspapers regarding the clean-up of the contaminated areas, and the possibility that contamination still exists in Minden. The EPA is investigating.

The Arbuckle Creek continued to overflow numerous times. In 2001, the town endured another flood with waters higher than the flood of 1956.

In 2015, Minden was annexed into the city of Oak Hill. A court battle ensued, but the annexation was upheld by the West Virginia Supreme Court of Appeals in November 2016.

Current day Minden is a small and economically depressed community of homes. The per capita income is low. The community and its members continue to endure hardships and heartaches.

Minden near the center of town behind the company store area.

Minden Company Store. The first company store in Minden was built by W.P. Rend in 1900. By 1927, this store was torn down and a larger store was built by the New River & Pocahontas Consolidated Coal Company. The two-story brick building even had a loading dock and an elevator.

Minden Company Store

The company store provided all supplies needed by the miners and their families, including fresh meat, groceries, household items, mining equipment, furniture, tools, toys, clothes, appliances and coffins. Items had excellent quality. On the left side of the store was the malt shop opened only on Sunday afternoons. The company store also offered advance credit to the miners. Scrip (money) was available in coins and paper.

When thinking of a company store, many of us automatically think of the song, "Sixteen Tons," popularly recorded by Tennessee Ernie Ford in 1955. The song was first recorded by Merle Travis in 1946.

Daddy, who listened to the radio every evening, was familiar with the song even when Merle Travis sang it, and often said that he was not going to "owe his soul to the company store." Usually, if our family couldn't afford it, we didn't get it.

Today I collect scrip coins. I have several from my youth which I cherish as well as others collected in later years.

The company store in Minden no longer stands. It burned down in May 1978.

Minden Community Church. The first church building was erected in Minden in 1907 built by the New River & Pocahontas Coal Company on land donated by William D. Thurmond. This church was originally called Minden Union Church and later called Minden Community Church.

The church still stands in a central portion of Minden, near where the company store once located. A group of caring former residents of Minden who have love and passion for the church joined together as a Committee to organize its restoration. Thanks to their persistence and dedicated efforts, the restoration is complete, and the town now has a Minden Community Meeting Center. This center is used for town functions including reunions, weddings, funerals, community meetings, and church revivals.

Minden Community Church during restoration.
Pictures courtesy of Minden Reunion 2005.

The Committee members who donated their time and energy are Jesse Bibb, Frank Hartenstein, Herbert Jones, Vivian Jones, Ray McClung, Lucille Burgess McClung, Dewey Pittman, Bill Ripoll, Paquita Ripoll Sarver, Kenneth Sarver and Phyllis Evans Scarbrough.

EPILOGUE

People of Minden

"Creeks can't talk, and mountains can't whisper, but if they could what stories would they tell of Minden in the older days when life was fresh and young, when coal cars rumbled along dusty tracks, when neighbors gathered for a talk at the fences, when children played in the streets and when slate dumps spilled their blackness over the hills."

By: Dewey Pittman
(Reunion – Minden, WV, 1905-2005)

Dewey B. Pittman. Dewey was born and raised in Minden, a son to Dempsey Pittman, a coal miner, and Mary Josie Drake. As an adult, the 6 ft. 2-inch blond young man became a teacher working for Fayette County Schools. He lived in Oak Hill. He spent numerous time and energy with the folks of Minden assisting with the youth groups with special interest in writing and photography. Dewey had active roles in the Minden Reunion as well as the restoration of the Minden Community Church. He always had an abundance of lively stories to tell of the earlier days of Minden.

Officers of Minden Local Union 5949, United Mine Workers of America

(Elected July 1955 for Two-Year Term)

President: George Crouch
Vice President: Charles H. Leach
Recording Secretary: A. M. Kelley
Financial Secretary: J. N. Dotson
Treasurer: Russell Cox
Trustees: Herbert Walker, Thomas Pryor and Columbus Barrett
Mine Committee: Casto Malines, William Waters and George
    Crouch
Safety Committee: Charles H. Leach and Thomas Pryor
Checkweighman: Herbert Walker
Doorkeeper: Henry Dixon

(Post-Herald and Register Newspaper, *Beckley, West Virginia, July 17, 1955)*

Rock Lick and Minden Elementary School

1957 – 1958
Teachers and Home Room Mothers and PTA Officers

PTA Officers:

President:	Mr. John Vegh
Vice President:	Mrs. Pauline Evans
Secretary:	Mrs. Elizabeth (Lizzy) Crone
Treasurer:	Mrs. James Walker

School Principal: Mr. R. W. Williams

Teacher: Mrs. Vivian Krause
Home Room Mothers: Mrs. June Pittman
                         Mrs. Carrie McCarthy

Teacher: Mrs. Leona Cavendish
Home Room Mothers: Mrs. John Vegh
                         Mrs. Ben Dixon

Teacher: Mrs. Greta Godsey
Home Room Mothers: Mrs. June Grabosky
                         Mrs. Annadean Lemaster

Teacher: Mrs. Lillian Rapp
Home Room Mothers: Mrs. Virginia Allen
                         Mrs. Pauline Evans

Teacher: Mrs. Jackson

Home Room Mothers:	Mrs. Nannie Harrah
	Mrs. Robert Simmerman
Teacher:	Mrs. Alice Morton
Home Room Mothers:	Mrs. Lizzie Crone
	Mrs. Chuyka
Teacher:	Mrs. Ella Miller
Home Room Mothers:	Mrs. Helen Crouch
	Mrs. James Walker
Teacher:	Mrs. Blake
Home Room Mothers:	Mrs. Arminto Dalton

(From the Parent Teachers Association's Records.)

Rock Lick and Minden Elementary School

1958 – 1959
Teachers and Home Room Mothers and PTA Officers

PTA Officers:
President: Mr. John Vegh
Vice President: Mrs. Pauline Evans
Secretary: Mrs. Elizabeth (Lizzy) Crone
Treasurer: Mrs. James Walker

School Principal: Mr. R. W. Williams

Teacher: Mrs. Leona Cavendish
Home Room Mothers: Mrs. Anna Wills
                               Mrs. Harmon
                               Mrs. Irene Blake
                               Mrs. Margaret Dixon

Teacher: Miss Carter
Home Room Mothers: Mrs. John Vegh
                               Mrs. Ben Dixon
                               Mrs. Burdette

Teacher: Mrs. Moak
Home Room Mothers: Mrs. Holt
                               Mrs. Ira Huffman
                               Mrs. Rodgers

Teacher: Mrs. Greta Godsey

Home Room Mothers:	Mrs. Becky Rainey
	Mrs. June Comer
	Mrs. Clyde McCarty
Teacher:	Mrs. Lillian Rapp
Home Room Mothers:	Mrs. June Grabosky
	Mrs. Scarbro
	Mrs. Chuyka
Teacher:	Mrs. Ruth Blake
Home Room Mothers:	Mrs. Dalton Dixon
	Mrs. Blevens
	Mrs. Pauline Evans
Teacher:	Mrs. Russell James
Home Room Mothers:	Mrs. Henry Dixon
	Mrs. Virginia Allen
Teacher:	Mrs. Alice Morton
Home Room Mothers:	Mrs. Plumb
	Mrs. Thorn
Teacher:	Mr. Andrew Wooten
Home Room Mothers:	Mrs. James Walker
	Mrs. Buster Crone

(From the Parent Teachers Association's Records.)

* * * * *

"Memories of a Lifetime"

"Every summer, the coal cars were left on the tracks across the creek in front of our house. That was a new playground for us. We would slide down the chutes, climb the ladders, take chalk and write our names on the inside and draw pictures. We got black as coal. I still don't know how my mother got all that coal dirt off us. Maybe she didn't, as we only took baths once a week and that was on Sunday nights. We never had hot water in our houses then, so Mom would have to heat the water on the wood stove in several pans and poured it in a galvanized tub for us to take baths. Six kids had to take turns taking a bath. The youngest was usually the last one.

When I was about 11 years old, a young man showed up at our door one day and said that he was told there was a young girl who could sing and play the guitar. My mom said that would be me. They wanted me to audition for a band called "Eddie Seacrist and the Rolling Rockets". They played in local clubs. My mother said she would chaperon me, so we went uptown to one of the clubs to audition. While I was waiting, this old drunk man came over and offered me money. I told my mother that I really didn't want to do this. After that, the Dunn Sisters asked me to sing with them in church, so I did that instead. Gospel music is still my favorite."

By: Sharon Stover van Buren, Minden Coal Camp Youngster

* * * * *

As told to me by Ruth Light Vegh. Ruth worked in the business office at the Minden Company Store for almost two years and was paid $350.00 a month. She married Andy Vegh, a fire boss at the Minden mines.

Ruth continued telling me, "Today, we hear of people living paycheck to paycheck, but many miners lived next paycheck to next paycheck. The miners were paid bi-monthly. Remember the song lyrics "I Owe My Soul to the Company Store" by Tennessee Ernie Ford? This is the reason why. If miners ran out of money, they could get scrip books on credit for $2.00, $5.00, $10.00 or $20.00. The money that was basically borrowed would come out of their next paychecks."

The company store was bustling on pay days because many miners and their families came into the store to buy scrip books on their next pay day. They could buy food, clothes and gasoline using these scrip books.

The miners that wished to purchase big items like furniture, appliances, and feed could open a charge account and pay so much a month until their account was paid in full. There was no interest charged for buying scrip books or opening charge accounts according to Ruth.

Ruth informed me that when the mines closed, many of the miners moved to Jackson County to work at the Kaiser Aluminum Plant near Ravenswood, West Virginia. "We were one of those families" says Ruth. "Even though we moved to a new area, it was not like starting over as far as friends and acquaintances were concerned since many had moved to the same area. Andy's brother John Vegh and his family also moved to Ravenswood and worked at this plant."

By: Ruth Light Vegh
Married to Andrew Vegh, Jr. who was raised in Minden and a coal miner in Minden.

* * * * *

As told to me by Lillian Vegh Phillips. Lillian, the youngest child of seven, was born in the town of Minden and lived there until her seventh grade of school when her family moved to Oak Hill. Lillian's dad, Andrew Vegh, was a coal miner of Minden having settled there after his arrival in this country from Hungary.

After marriage to Carl Phillips, Lillian returned to Minden in 1956. Homes were being sold at reasonable rates with payment plans so she and Carl excitedly purchased their first home.

Lillian began working for the Arbuckle Public Service District in Minden when it was established in 1976, initially being the only office staff, and worked there until she retired.

Prior to that she states, *"Minden's water source came from springs nearby the mines. The water would be pumped. We only had to pay a flat rate of $4.00 for water no matter what we used. But after the mines closed, the water was often dirty and off a lot. We would have to fill tubs full of water just in case the water was off."*

She continues telling me that a committee was formed of twelve men, one being her husband Carl Phillips. This committee knew of a water source in Conchu which could service the town, but they needed financial means. Arbuckle Public Service District was formed, and a loan was obtained in 1976. Individual homes were metered, and water fees charged by usage. This water supplied Minden, Lock Lick, Conchu and Old Minden Road. This water company was recently sold.

Arbuckle Public Service District also established and maintained a sewage system for Minden in 1979 acquiring another loan. Prior to that, there was no sewer system for Minden, Rock Lick and Conchu. Fees for sewer are based on water consumption. According to Lillian, this sewer system located in Conchu maintains the sewage system with pump stations and services not only Minden but other nearby areas.

Lillian also was a member of the Minden Garden Club where she has many fond memories. *"We popped popcorn and would string them and cranberries and put them in trees for the birds. We encouraged families to care for their yards by giving prizes for best decorated yard during the holidays and best decorated door. We cared about our community."*

She stated that the clean-up of the old Minden cemetery was one of their projects. Other members of the Garden Club that Lillian remembered are Lizzy Crone, Ann Miller, Henrietta Brellahan, Ann Watters, Loupy Dixon, Jean Dixon, Lucille Miller and Pauline Evans.

Lillian and Carl eventually moved from Minden to a house in nearby Oak Hill, where she continues to reside.

Spirit of the Miner

Their lives were lost in a place so low,
We wonder what must become of their soul,
When tragedy comes and love ones go,
We grieve many years wanting to know,
The day when a blast occurs there,
Or the top cracks and caves in where,
The miner is working so dark and dank,
Makes us wonder what they felt, would think,
My life may be at hand this day,
What will my wife, children, and family say,
to my leaving them when I came to work today,
To earn a living for food and a place for them to stay,
So, to the lost miner let's continue to pray...

Billy Bibb (9871)

Billy Bibb was born and raised in Minden. He has written numerous poems that are unpublished reflecting his life as a child growing up in Minden. (Contribution by Billy Bibb)

Minden and Rock Lick School Students 1958 – 1959. (School pictures of all students during this year may not be displayed.)

Minden and Rock Lick School Students 1958 – 1959. (School pictures of all students during this year may not be displayed.)

ACKNOWLEDGEMENTS

A special thanks to Christy Steele Frazer for editing.

Reading by John "J.J." Michael Frazer.

Interviews and contributions from Gene "Squeaky" Crone, Charles Crone, Robert Crone and John Crone.

Tape recording interview with Reginald Buster Crone and Elizabeth Vegh Crone conducted by Sue Crone Mundy.

Scrapbook of Elizabeth "Lizzy" Vegh Crone.

Interview and contribution by Lillian Vegh Phillips.

Interview and contribution by Ruth Light Vegh.

Contribution by Sharon Stover van Buren

Information and pictures courtesy of Jane Webb Terry.

Information by Dalton (Nune) Dixon.

Pictures courtesy of Scott Crone.

Pictures courtesy of Rebecca Crone.

Contribution of memories by Paquita Ripoll Sarver.

Contribution of memories by Bill Harmon.

Contribution by Billy Bibb.

Picture courtesy of Sharon Stover van Buren.

Pictures courtesy of Betty Potter Michalski.

History of Fayette County West Virginia by J. T. Peters and H. B. Carden, Jarrett Printing Company, 1926.

Church History by Ray McClung, 1998.

Minden First One Hundred Years and Minden Memories, http://westvirginiatopcities.com.

Year 1907; Arrival: New York, New York; Microfilm Serial: T715, 1897-1957; Microfilm Roll: Roll 0946; Line 25; Page Number: 143 and Year: 1913; Roll 2075; Line 29; Page Number:71).

Ancestry.com

The Fayette Tribune, Minden & Rock Lick, By Mrs. Buster Crone and *Minden News, By Mrs. Buster Crone* and *Minden Mailbox,* Oak Hill, WV.

The Fayette Tribune Newspaper, Commission Hears Concern Regarding Minden Annexation.

The Fayette Tribune, *By Sarah Plummer, Mar 23, 2017,* Residents *at sewer project hearing raise concerns about Minden superfund site,*

Post Herald and Register, Beckley, WV, *Floodwaters Cause $75,000 to $125,000 Damage at Minden,* July 29, 1956 and *Normally Placid Arbuckle Creek Rampages Through Oak Hill and Minden After Yesterday's*

Storms, July 28, 1956 and Hit by Flood, July 29, 1956; and *Crouch Re-Elected Minden Union Head,* July 17, 1955.

U.S. School Yearbooks, Years 1958, 1959.

<u>Raleigh Register</u>, Beckley, W.V. *Officers of Minden Local Union 5949, United Mine Workers of America, July 17, 1955;* and *DAR Honors Collins Student,* May 20, 1958 and David Refuses to *Comment on Mines Closure,* July 21, 1959 and *Minden Fire Damage Figured at $3,000,* Feb. 17, 1956 and *Happy Blackburn,* Feb._27, 1958 and advertisement by Blackburn Patteson Realty Co., June 29, 1956, July 2, 1956, Feb. 27, 1958.

<u>The Register-Herald</u>, June 25, 2017, By Jessica Farrish, *Former Shaffer employee: "A lot of people died because I dumped that stuff."*

Minden, WV 1905 – 2005, Town Reunion CD produced and narrated by Dewey Pittman.

About Montgomery West Virginia, By Frances Susan Crone and Robert Kelvin Holliday, <u>The Montgomery Herald, Inc.</u>, Montgomery, 1958.

Minden and Rock Lick PTA Meetings, 1955, 1956, 1957, 1958 and 1959.

Year: *1920*; Census Place: *Fayetteville, Fayette, West Virginia*; Roll: *T625_1947*; Page: *15A*; Enumeration District: *15*; Image: *734.*

Year: *1930*; Census Place: *Fayetteville, Fayette, West Virginia*; Roll: *2531*; Page: *27A*; Enumeration District: *0014*; Image: *801.0*; FHL microfilm: *2342265.*

Year: *1940*; Census Place: *Fayetteville, Fayette, West Virginia*; Roll: *T627_4401*; Page: *18B*; Enumeration District: *10-17.*

U.S. v. Shaffer Equipment Co., Nos. 92-2024, 93-1007, and 93-1049, United States Court of Appeals, Fourth Circuit. Argued May 4, 1993. Decided December 9, 1993.

Centennial Celebration First One Hundred Years, Minden, West Virginia, 1905 - 2005 by Sharon Watkins Conner, Postmaster at Minden.

Minden, WV, Reunion, 1988 by Jerry Bryant, Published March 5, 2014.

Printed in the United States
By Bookmasters